for every child who dreams of going to school

PENGUIN ENTERPRISE

Penguin Books India (P) Ltd., 11 Community Centre, Panchsheel Park, New Delhi 110 017, India
Penguin Books Ltd., 80 Strand, London WC2R ORL, UK
Penguin Group Inc., 375 Hudson Street, New York, NY 10014, USA
Penguin Books Australia Ltd., 250 Camberwell Road, Camberwell, Victoria 3124, Australia
Penguin Books Canada Ltd., 10 Alcorn Avenue, Suite 300, Toronto, Ontario, M4V 3B2, Canada
Penguin Books (NZ) Ltd., Cnr Rosedale and Airbourne Roads, Albany, Auckland, New Zealand
Penguin Books South Africa Pty. Ltd., 24 Sturdee Avenue, Rosebank 2196, South Africa

First published in Penguin Enterprise by Penguin Books India 2003

Printed at Ajanta Offset, New Delhi

For sale in India only

PENGUIN ENTERPRISE

Penguin Books India (P) Ltd., 11 Community Centre, Panchsheel Park, New Delhi 110 017, India
Penguin Books Ltd., 80 Strand, London WC2R ORL, UK
Penguin Group Inc., 375 Hudson Street, New York, NY 10014, USA
Penguin Books Australia Ltd., 250 Camberwell Road, Camberwell, Victoria 3124, Australia
Penguin Books Canada Ltd., 10 Alcorn Avenue, Suite 300, Toronto, Ontario, M4V 3B2, Canada
Penguin Books (NZ) Ltd., Cnr Rosedale and Airbourne Roads, Albany, Auckland, New Zealand
Penguin Books South Africa Pty. Ltd., 24 Sturdee Avenue, Rosebank 2196, South Africa

First published in Penguin Enterprise by Penguin Books India 2003

Printed at Ajanta Offset, New Delhi

For sale in India only

city classrooms, mountain fields, desert tents and glowing temples.
and waiting for buses on chaotic street corners, they come with

black-buckle shoes, barefoot, in their uniforms. They come because
school can change their lives.
of children do not go to school in India.

has the right to participate in lessons that can change their lives.
fun and helps them to become who they want to be. And every child
going to school, if they could — we just have to ask.
school can be, from kids to kids, to you and me.

possible by the Bharti Foundation. bharti

Bharti Enterprises, India's largest private telecom company,
improve the quality of their lives through education
to society as a whole. Going to School in India represents
schools and organisations, many religions and diverse kids
kids to kids who go to government and private schools. Through
Bharti Foundation communicates a world of possibilities for the
future of India... our children.

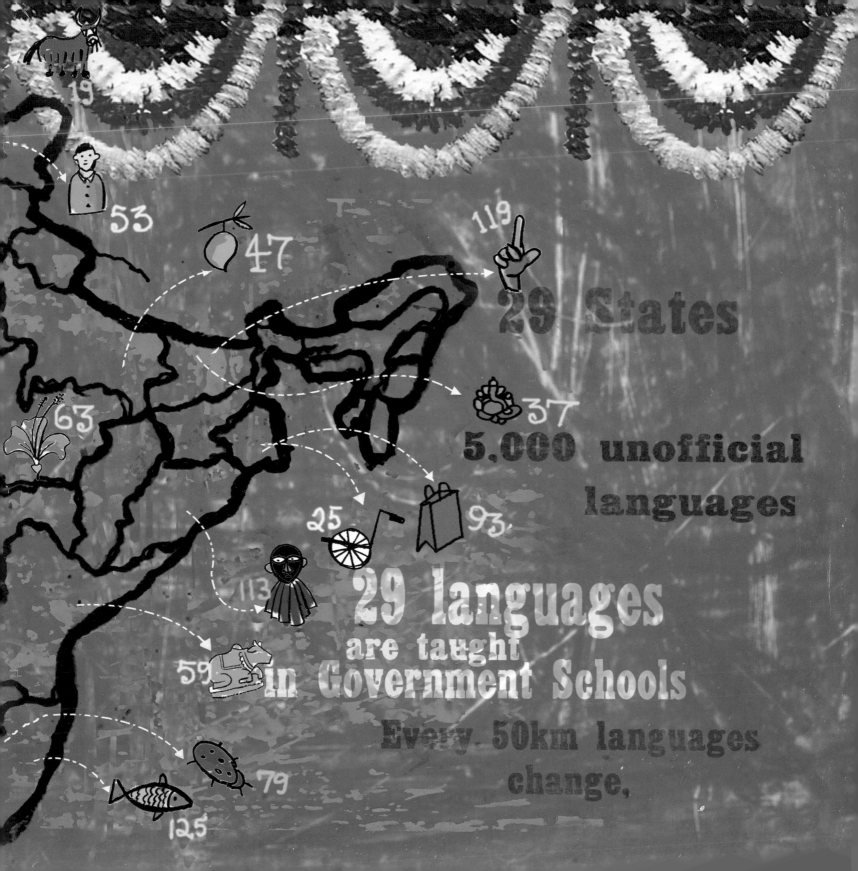

19

53

47

119

29 States

63

37

5,000 unofficial languages

25

93

113

29 languages are taught in Government Schools

59

Every 50km languages change,

79

12,5

Getting to school in India is a wild ride. Every school day, millions of children climb into school buses, sit on each other's laps in cycle-rickshaws, walk along the edge of mountains, cross scorching deserts on rickety bicycles and swing across raging blue rivers on dangling rope swings – just to get to school. Against great odds they come, because they believe going to school can change their lives, and if it does, it was certainly worth the ride.

Getting to school

Rope Bridge, Nagaland

Nagaland is a mountainous state of entangled rainforests. In remote areas, only blowing bridges provide a way for kids to get to school. Carrying school bags woven from tribal cloth, children place their bag straps on their heads, keeping their hands free to hold on to the ropes to keep their balance.

Vallam, Kerala

Crossing over water is a cautious step. Carefully into Vallams, or boats made of solid wood, and oarsmen row the boys across the still waters to school.

Rope Swing, Ladakh

Hundreds of feet above the glass-blue river below, Ladakhi kids climb into an iron rope swing with a giant rusted pulley and a well-woven rope. Spalzes Angmo, age 10, reaches up, pulls the rope through the pulley and edges their swing out over the drop – whirling across the raging river. Arriving at the other side the kids strap on their backpacks and climb two more kilometres uphill, to get to school.

inspiring lessons

lessons that make you want to go to school

'Prayer flags are for God who comes in the wind to blow through them,' whispers Tsewang Gurmet, age 10, looking up from colouring a line of brightly dancing prayer flags. 'God is in the wind,' he says, placing a hand on his chest, where his heart would be, 'and in my heart.'

18

Government Primary School, Tukla Village, Leh district, Ladakh, Jammu & Kashmir.
Save the Children UK.

prayer flags

Y IS FOR YAK

Monastery

19

Stanzin Kongo, age 8, wearing his crimson red sweater and grey trousers, weaves along a footpath on the edge of a vast mountain. Followed by five boys wearing the same school uniform, Stanzin and his friends move together like a fluid red stream racing up instead of down. Up and up they climb, cheeks shiny red from the cold. Some rough little feet wear flip-flops, others stumble in dusty, round-toed black shoes. Chatting to each other in Ladakhi, the boys climb higher and higher into the sky.

Going to school in a mountain village means you have to be able to climb. Stanzin knows how to climb, in fact all of his friends do, it is how they get to school. Jeeps can go no further than the road – and from the road they choose a path upwards for two kilometres until they reach a plateau on the side of a mountain to find their government school. There is no electricity in this school or in the village, but in the summer months this does not matter – school moves outside where there is plenty of light. Today, high in the mountains where India touches Tibet, 29 kids are learning English in the bright, cold sunlight.

Stanzin

The sky in Ladakh is electric blue, as blue as the river that is as cold as ice, and the rocks are pale white. Ladakh is a high altitude desert. Ladakhis say this is where the earth meets the sky.

'Y is for YAK,' Stanzin exclaims, plopping himself down on the red carpet that most surely should be able to fly into the great, blue sky. Stanzin is thumbing through a pack of cards* that have pictures of Ladakhi queens and black yaks, which everyone knows well. The cards help the kids learn new English words.

Stanzin holds the black, furry YAK in his chapped hands. 'Y,' Stanzin tastes the letter, listening to the acoustics of Y play in the wind. 'Yaks climb,' explains Stanzin as he blows his nose – mountain winds tend to make your nose run. Stuffing his large polka-dotted handkerchief into his shallow pocket, Stanzin continues chatting about yaks – it seems he actually has one at home. 'My favourite thing in the whole world is my yak, Rokpo. Who makes noises like Rrrrrrrrrrrr,' Stanzin says rolling 'R' from the back of his mouth. 'I ride on my yak, but not alone, someone has to help me because he is quite big and gets angry.' Stanzin puts two fists to his head to show a yak's horns. 'My yak is big, black and full of thick hair. You need about five of me to make one yak!' And to show you exactly what he means, Stanzin's five friends line up to make a yak. Getting ready to spin the yak into motion racing around their mountain playground, the boys' feet stamp and stomp the dusty ground, but Stanzin stalls the yak's take off with a yell: 'Wait for the tail!'

Carma, age 3, who comes to school because he wants to, races to catch up with his outstretched arm. He is the tail.

Tail ⟶

* SECMOL, an NGO based in Leh, developed picture cards of Ladakhi people, places and things to help children in Ladakh learn English.

igmat Chosket, age 10, watches the yak tear around her school in the sky. Waiting until the dust has settled, she shuffles forward on her knees holding a card showing a Ladakhi window with ornate carvings and delicately painted designs. 'WINDOW,' she says carefully tasting the foreign sounds, then in Ladakhi she explains swiftly, holding a drawing she has made: 'I live in a glass room which keeps me warm, it lets the heat in. From my room I can see my vegetable garden with radishes, turnips, carrots, cauliflowers and bright blue flowers. I like looking out of my window because at night I can see the stars.' Jigmat looks down at her dusty red uniform, and then out into the wind. 'Sometimes I'm afraid and sometimes I feel free.'

As Jigmat speaks the wind suddenly changes direction, and Stanzin's yak comes racing back, skidding onto the red rugs. Crayons are passed from hand to hand, and yaks of all shapes and sizes begin prancing along the bottom of everyone's pages.

'YAK YAK YAK,' Stanzin burbles as he draws.

'I can see yaks too from my window,' Jigmat smiles.

Jigmat

glass house

Jigmat Chosket
Class 4 Roll No. 2
TUKLa 10

has

22

Ladakh gets over 300 days of sunshine a year, which means you can even get sunburned in the winter.

'My school is made of stone, wood and mud. We have one classroom, one storeroom with two steel boxes of books and games, a football, a ring game and some skipping ropes. In the winter we keep warm with a firewood stove, but it is still cold. I go home for lunch because I live really close and there is no drinking water at school.' Tundup Namgil, age 10, Government Primary School Tukla, Tukla Village, Leh district, Ladakh.

23

HAIDER ON WHEELS

Haider Ali Molla, age 10, gets to school in his wheelchair.

Every morning, Haider's friends, Subid Ali, age 10, Saifur Ali Molla, age 13 and Kalam Sheik, age 10, arrive at Haider's house half an hour before school begins. Deciding who gets to push Haider today, they tip the wheelchair back onto its two big black wheels and are away.

Haider breathes in with a little difficulty, but smiles as he recounts his 'wheelie' trails. 'The road to school is not a good road, it has mud and gets flooded in the monsoon and there are lots of pot-holes.' Looking up at his friends, he smiles, 'Sometimes I have to ask them to go slowly please, because it's hard for me.'

Haider lives one kilometre away from Raspunja Free Primary School. One kilometre was a long way for Haider when he did not have wheels. In fact, one kilometre was so far that Haider didn't go to school until he was given a wheelchair. Now he wheels wherever the boys take him, and they take him everywhere.

In the beginning, Haider's mother was worried about sending him to school. She had many questions. 'How will he go to the toilet? Will he tell his friends he needs to go? Will he be embarrassed?' She shook her head and said 'no' to the friends who had brought Haider a wheelchair. She said 'no' to the idea that other boys would bring him to school.

But Sanchar did not give up. Instead they talked to everyone who could help Haider go to school. They talked to the teachers, they talked to the kids and they found three friends who would wheel Haider to school. Sanchar asked everyone to ask Haider to be a part of what was going on – whether they were about to have lunch or go to the toilet. 'Please ask Haider too,' they said. And they did.

98% of disabled children do not go to school in India. The Government of India passed the Persons with Disabilities Act stating that every child with a disability must have access to free education. But only when communities, families and friends help disabled children will children like Haider 'be able' to go to school. Disabled children just like their able-bodied friends, need a friendly environment to achieve their full potential — schools with ramps for wheelchairs, and teachers, parents and friends who understand what disabled children can do, and work with them so their dreams come true.

Saifur, a firm friend, explains what else Haider needed to go to school. 'We put a loop on his water bottle to hang it from the handle, and we strapped his backpack across the back of his wheelchair, and there is a mat inside of his backpack for sitting on the floor.' Saifur's hands rest on top of Haider's blue backpack, which the boys have placed behind him, to support him like a cushion, 'Haider goes to school everyday except when it's raining because he cannot hold an umbrella and we have a hard time pushing the wheelchair through the mud. When it really rains heavily and a lot, then none of us go to school.'

'In the holidays, Haider gets upset because he misses school — we have a Ludo game, so we go to his house and play that.'

Sitting small in his wheelchair, Haider dreams about what he will do when he is older. Grinning at his friends, he says, 'When I grow up I want to play football.'

Haider began to dream only after he started coming to school — all Haider needed to dream were great friends and some wheels.

What do you need to dream?

Raspunja Free Primary School, 24 Paraganas South, West Bengal. Sanchar.

'Shesh Naag, a snake who holds the world on his back, made the earthquake take place on 26 January so children would not be hurt. He knew that day children would not be in school, they would be outside in the fields marching in parades. He chose that day so children would not die. But many children did die when they ran home to see if their parents were safe.' Mahindra, age 12, wipes away a trickling line of sweat from his forehead, 'If we sin more, if people of different religions keep hurting each other and if we keep treating animals badly and eating them, the earthquake will come again.'

BUILDING MY HOUSE

Sitting next to a giant pile of rubble, once upon a time a government school, 32 mini-architects are designing houses they would like to live in. Weaving dreams out of the streaking shadows, these architects are building bright houses of mud, glass and straw. Glued and pasted together with dusty hands, houses with green doors, holes for windows, flat roofs and spiralling stairs emerge out of the rubble. As an architect, you have to be very careful building a house on shifting stone because you never know when the stones might move again.

Pratham, Biku Bhai's courtyard, Ram Nagri Slum, Bhuj, Gujarat 27

On 26 January 2001, Republic Day,* an earthquake measuring 7.5 on the Richter Scale shook Gujarat, destroying countless houses and burying thousands of people under stone. Biku Bhai lives next door to a pile of rubble which was once the children's school. For several weeks after the earthquake Biku Bhai watched the rubble, wondering. Weeks turned into months and his thought soon became an idea, then a question. Rather than have the children miss another day of school, would they like to come to school in his courtyard? Teachers from the government school agreed, and helped out by 'friends of children' from Pratham, children came to school, glad to be back together, glad to be away from their damaged homes. Even though the children sit outside in the scorching heat, they would rather sit in a place where there are no walls than go to school inside.

'The earth still moves like this,' says Lucky, age 8, holding her hands flat and moving them from side-to-side. More than a year after the earthquake the earth is still bending and stretching, healing and putting itself back together. Aftershocks rock Bhuj every day, making the ground beneath the children's feet tremble.

The children of Gujarat remember the day the earthquake came, it was a national holiday, usually celebrated by parades, no school and delicious sweets. But the earthquake came so suddenly, and destroyed so many lives, that many children wondered why it happened, and when there were no answers that seemed right, they found their own reasons. Vanit, age 9, takes a deep breath and explains, 'The goddess of the earth, Dharti Mata, felt the earth had become too heavy with sin, so she put it down. That is why the earth moved. But then the god Shankar who has a third eye and can see everything told Dharti Mata to pick up the world again. That is why everything is still now.'

Radha's House

28

* A national holiday in India, a celebration of the day India became a Republic.

'Shhhh,' whispers Shilpa, age 8, pulling up the sleeves of her worn, blue dress as she imitates the earth that still speaks in aftershocks of muted tones.

Still, calm. Now the earth is still enough to build houses, calm enough to go to school. And that is just what these kids are doing, constructing houses from their imagination, houses that will fit into their world and help them to come to terms with what they lost.

Shilpa has not built a house, but smoothening her hair back into a ponytail, she leaps up, to go visiting everyone else's creation.

Peering into Radha's house, Shilpa exclaims: 'It's a Kutchi house!' Shilpa is missing her front tooth, so her words escape with a whistle. Radha, age 9, carefully holds her traditional house at arm's length. It is just like the one she used to have with a triangular roof and mud walls. 'No one was hurt when our house fell down, but we lost our TV and we are still digging to find it. We had to sell all of our belongings to be able to build our new tin house.' With a dusty finger Radha traces the name she wrote on her roof, 'I made my house out of mud, cardboard and date leaves. I painted the wall purple and I put my name and my father's name on the roof so people would know how to find us.'

'I know where to find you,' Shilpa giggles, turning to let her fingers feel their way through the door of Paro's house.

Paro Vagri, age 7, is wearing a bright dress that matches her blue house. In Paro's house you can play games. 'We climb the ladder onto the roof to play cricket. There is enough room to bowl, but you might lose the ball over the side, and then you have to climb down and get it. We always argue about who has to go get the ball. Our house was like this but it collapsed and now we stay in a hut. We won't build this kind of house again because it gets destroyed in earthquakes.' With an open palm, Paro lightly supports the blue textured walls of her house and whispers to no one in particular: 'The earthquake came because people had been swearing too much.'

Paro's
House

29

Everyone's house has a story, a story of a house they dream of building, a story for the house they used to have. By building their houses children are breathing life into dreams, beginning to believe in possibility, and even imagining houses they have never seen.

Shilpa is almost at the end of her tour and she lies down flat on her stomach trying to see inside Puja's house. Smiling shyly, Puja picks up her brown paper house and places it under her arm, 'It needs glue.'

Shilpa smiles a wiggly-toothed grin, believing in what glue can do, 'My house cracked too, in the earthquake.' And then jumping up to tug on the sleeve of the photographer who is in the middle of taking Puja's photo, she asks:

'Has your house fallen down too?'

Puja's House

The Gujarat Earthquake destroyed an estimated 10,000 schools and 100,000 homes. Creative projects such as building model houses after yours has been destroyed, can help children who have experienced trauma, express their feelings.

30

GOING TO SCHOOL IN THE DARK

A solitary solar lantern casts blue shadows across the cracked white walls. Closing the wooden shutters to keep out the cold and to keep the girls warm inside, Devki, the Prime Minister of the Children's Parliament, sweeps through the room, sealing the door behind her. It is cold in the desert night.

Devki

Night Schools

In some dusty villages of Rajasthan, girls work during the day. When other children go to school, these girls stay home to look after their younger brothers and sisters. As the sun sets and their household work ends, they emerge from their houses to walk each other to school in the fading light. Night schools give girls a chance to go to school after their household work is done.

32

Night School, Rampura Village, Ajmer District, Rajasthan. SWRC Tilonia. Plan International HIVOS Netherlands, German Agro Action Germany, UNESCO Paris, Ministry of Education Govt of India.

Without saying a word, she wraps her worn beige shawl tightly around her shoulders and finds a place to sit in the folding darkness. Devki is 13 years old, but she seems much older. Maybe this is because her life is so full: Devki works at home during the day feeding cows and buffalos, and walks several kilometres to collect water from the hand-pump, and at night she works too, as Prime Minister. Devki has a lot of responsibility for a girl who is only 13.

Devki leans forward, her finger tracing Hindi questions in her notebook. She seems to prefer listening to speaking. 'Is there too little light?' she asks the 42 girls sitting in the shadows. The girls nod. It is hard to see, even harder to read. A little girl yawns in the blue, reflected light. 'Electricity is a problem,' Devki says, watching two more fluorescent solar lanterns arrive in the room. 'Light comes and goes, so we have to make our own from solar batteries. Each night school has a solar tube light, but they are not very strong, so we need lanterns to see. If there is no light, we sit in darkness.' Devki shrugs, 'That's all right too, we sing when we sit in the dark.'

During the day, solar lanterns store energy from the harsh desert sun, and at night they light the night schools with a fluorescent, ghostly light.

Bal Sansad

This Children's Parliament was created so every girl who goes to school in the dark would have a chance to learn how a parliament works. Every other year 3,000 girls vote to elect the members of parliament. Devki was elected last year and she will serve as Prime Minister for two years. As Prime Minister, Devki, with her cabinet of ministers, has to ensure that the 150 night schools across the district are running well. And the only way to make sure is for Devki to visit each school, as she is doing tonight.

33

Concentrating in the sharp light, Devki watches the girls fold newspapers in all directions. 'It is our school, so we decide what we want to learn,' she says, explaining why newspaper hats of all shapes and sizes are emerging from the darkness. Devki begins to fold a sheet of coloured newspaper as she tells the story of how she came to be Prime Minister. 'I knew I wanted to do something for children, so I thought the parliament was the best way. I went to each night school and met the girls in the school and asked them to vote for me. I told them: 'If you do not have enough paper or if you need new carpets to sit on, I will mention it in the meetings and make sure you get it'.' Devki's eyes glisten in the night-light as she explains with a half-smile, both pleased and shy at the same time, 'The girls chose me.'

Out of the darkness, a small girl hands Devki a folded hat. Devki is tired from her long day at work, but to make her dream of opening more night schools come true, she needs to ask more questions. 'Who lives next to someone who does not go to school?' Hands go up, hats rustle. 'If you know someone who does not go to school, can you bring them with you next time?' Everyone nods, but a few girls turn around to watch the door. Santosh, age 13, a minister in Devki's cabinet, has arrived.

Santosh is standing shyly next to a smiling man wearing a brown woolen scarf. Devki nods and starts to ask another question, but the girls are no longer listening. They are watching the smiling man step quietly through them, disappearing behind a blackboard in the corner of the room. Suddenly a puppet with a large moustache and bright red Rajasthani turban pops up from behind the blackboard, whirling his head wildly from side to side. Devki rocks back on her heels, knowing her questions will have to wait for another night. 'Yoo hoo, Santosh, How OLD are YOU?' the puppet yells. Santosh picks up her long purple skirt to step through the crowd, shyly looking up at the bobbing puppet.

'13,' she whispers. 'Is that 7 and 9?' the puppet asks. Santosh shakes her head. 'No.' '9 and 12?'

Santosh shakes her head more furiously. '13,' she whispers, '13.' SMACK, the puppet kisses Santosh, making the room explode in laughter.

'Now kiss me, I kissed you!' the puppet insists, offering his cheek. As Santosh reaches up to return the kiss Devki wraps her shawl tightly around her shoulders and disappears into the cold dark night. She still has another school to visit tonight.

Santosh

Stepping barefoot onto sacred ground, an elderly woman walks slowly into the temple, carrying a glowing oil lamp in her cupped hands. Placing her candle down on the smooth stone floor, she barely notices the children sitting cross-legged between the blue-green pillars going to school.

Pratham, Shiv Mandir, Bhadra Ghat, Patna, Bihar

As more visitors step through the corridors of the temple, more children arrive, slipping off their shoes and rolling their yellow mats out on the warm, stone floor. Leaving their shoes in a perfect line where the yellow mats begin, the children quietly fold one leg over another to sit down on the floor. Touching their thumbs to index fingers, resting their open hands on their knees, they close their eyes. School in this temple begins very quietly.

'OM,' hums Ravi Kant, age 9, opening one eye and tasting the sound, as he keeps the other eye closed. 'OM is a sound made before and after Yoga,' whispers Ravi quietly feeling the vibrations move across his lips. OM echoes through the temple as Ravi opens both eyes, revealing a face as bright as the sun. 'We start with Sukhasana.* It's Yoga,' Ravi says, ironing his mint green t-shirt with his hands. 'Sukhasana means 'easy sitting pose' – it is the first asana* we do in the morning.' Blowing their stomachs up like balloons, the children inhale, and slowly releasing their breaths, they bring their stomachs back to normal size. Ravi looks relieved as he puffs out a great breath, 'It's for feeling what you have inside.'

* 'Sukh' means relaxed, and 'asana'…
* Asana: Yoga positions are called asanas. There are over 84,000 asanas based on living creatures (or things) in our world – the idea is to move through all of the positions – scorpion, peacock, locust, crow – until you reach the last one, which is you – a human.

38

The sound of falling rain breaks the children's silence – rainmaking yoga has begun. Eyes tightly shut, imagining the coming monsoon,* the children tap their first fingers lightly on the palms of their hands; rain is just beginning to fall. Then two fingers tap slightly harder – it is drizzling, three fingers – it is raining, four fingers – it's pouring and five – clapping as hard as they can at different times, they make lightning, thunder, even a storm. Ravi opens his eyes. 'Then we go back the other way until the rain has finished and the sun comes out.'

A few more raindrops splatter on open hands.
'Rain is good because trees can grow,' Ravi says, lifting his right leg up to balance on the inside of his left knee. And so the children begin their last Yoga stretch Vrksasana,* balancing their bodies and thoughts to become trees, growing strong in a temple.

Traditionally whenever schools were being repaired children and teachers moved into temples to continue going to school. Temples are public property, which means they belong to everyone, anyone can go inside and there is always fresh, running water. In crowded cities sometimes temples are the only space left where new schools can be opened so kids can learn all that they need to enroll in formal school. Although it's a Hindu temple, most of the children who go to school here are Muslim. Like anyone who moves from one place to another, it is hard to fit in at first, this school builds a friendly bridge into the formal school.

Ravi

* Monsoon, the rains that wash India each summer, flooding city streets and reviving parched fields.
* 'Vrksasana' pronounced, 'Rikshasana' is the Yogic tree pose.

WACKY PROJECTS @ WORK

A small boys wish

40

Ornate wrought-iron gates swing open wide on their well-oiled hinges to welcome you inside. It's open day at St. Mary's and everyone from grandparents to parents, sisters and brothers have come to see the extraordinary models the boys have built. The challenge posed to the boys was brief: be innovative, create models that can help you and others learn 'by doing', and try to make your models come alive so everyone will want to learn more. And with that the boys went to work, letting their imaginations soar, delving into subjects that had always intrigued them but which they had not yet had a chance to learn.

Ambling through St. Mary's great iron gates, boys from Al Madrasa Tus Saifiya Tul Buchaniyah School have come to see just how innovative the St. Mary's boys can be.

Ahmed

St. Mary's ICSE High School, Mazagaon, Mumbai, Maharashtra.

41

Exploding Volcanoes

In a classroom at the end of a creaking-wooden-floored hall, Jai Sarvaiya, age 10, stands on tiptoes peering into the top of his volcano. Noticing you have paused at his stall, he adjusts his tie, 'To explode the volcano, we put potassium permanganate and glycerine together, and then it is supposed to start smoking by itself.' Jai looks at his volcano – there is no smoke, and so Jai keeps talking as he searches for his matchbox in the pockets of his white uniform shorts. Ahmed Ali, age 13, from Al Madrasa, peeps through his line of quiet friends wearing their blue and white kurta uniforms.

Jai

'If it does not catch fire by itself, you light it,' Jai says, striking a match and reaching into the volcano. Strike one – no smoke. Jai looks bewildered and tries again – strike two, no luck yet, and now his audience is getting restless. Holding his breath and wishing hard, Jai tries one last time. Strike three, this time he is rewarded, for after a moment smoke slowly begins to rise. **Poof!** The volcano explodes. Ahmed smiles, impressed; as his friends move away to a safer distance, he holds his ground, intrigued. **Poof! Poof!** The volcano explodes again and again. Flinging handfuls of dirt into the volcano, Jai and his friends anxiously try to extinguish the happily exploding model.

'We wanted to make a volcano to show you how the world erupts,' explains Mayuraj Deshmukh, age 10, wielding another handful of dirt. 'But we didn't know it would'nt go out.'

Ahmed adds a little more dirt to the smoke, flashes Mayuraj a shy smile and races to catch up with his friends who have moved onto a wired solar-bulb system.

Light Fantastic Solar-System

Welcoming you to his stall like a ringmaster at a circus, Anuj Solanki, age 10, twists two red wires together bringing his solar system to life. 'The sun is the brightest thing we can see in the universe! It's right in the middle, the most important star that everything else goes around, so we chose a bright bulb so it would shine the brightest. Then we soldered each planet to the others by wires and attached one wire that links half of the solar system to one battery, and the other bit of the solar system to the other battery.'

Anuj fiddles with the wires and his sun blinks on and off. 'The whole solar system on one battery would not have worked. It would be like everyone in Bombay living off one electricity meter. Sooner or later you would get the smell of smoke when your system busts up.' Tickled by the thought, Anuj carries on explaining his love for electricity. 'I have been playing with switches, wires and plugs since I was very small. I was always opening up toys to see how they worked.'

Ahmed holds his face in his hands, considers Anuj's wires and asks the first question from the line of visiting boys: 'Would you like to visit another planet?'

Anuj answers matter-of-factly as if this electrical scientist has all he needs. 'We are happy on earth and don't want to visit any other place'; and then ending his three-ring circus with a quiet finale: 'Plus it would be too hot, don't you think?'

Ahmed nods, his right hand reaching up quickly to secure his round, white cap that was beginning to slip to one side.

43

Steaming Factory Smoke

'Why incense sticks?' Ahmed asks Johan Rerprira, age 10, half-hidden by the perfumed smoke rising from the roof of his factory; coughing slightly, Johan considers his choice. 'Factories should make clothes and things without making smoke. Smoke affects other people's lives around a factory.'

Ahmed nods, and Smeet Shah, age 10, appears out of Johan's smoke with the air of a superstar playing a cameo role: 'This factory makes pollution. There are cows who don't. We should go back to that!'

Ahmed laughs with Smeet, and once more the Al Madrasa boys move on, this time to the top of the world.

Nishant's hands

The Cold North

Nilay Yogesh, age 11, forgets to say hello because he's a little nervous. He begins by pointing to the dry grape stem covered with cotton: 'In the cold north trees don't have leaves, and are always covered with snow, and they are cone shaped so the snow can fall off.' Nilay breathes in heavily – relieved the first part is over: 'In the cold north people lived in igloos and traded fish and sealskins; they used dogs for riding in olden times, but now they use snowmobiles and in the summer they used kayaks to get to school.'

'No they didn't!' interrupts Nishant Bharat, age 11. Nishant has been quietly rubbing two pieces of styrofoam together, making snow fall on their cold north. But now he objects: 'They did not go to school at all, it was too cold!'

Nilay is visibly shocked by this eruption from his once quiet snow-blower, and gathering himself together, reasserts: 'But now they do, now the modern school is all heated, now there are oil-drilling factories.'

Ahmed softly touches the grape stem covered with cotton and whispers in confidence to Nishant, 'It really does look like a tree.' Pleased that Ahmed thinks their tree does in fact look like a tree, Nishant decides to play again, and resumes rubbing his styrofoam pieces together to make snow fall once again.

Factory smoke

Fresh Air
Grow More Trees

SIYARAM MILLS

45

Extending her gnarled, leafy arms as far
as she can, the magnificent mango tree casts a
giant shadow across the brushed, earthy ground. Swaying
inquisitively in the breeze, the lush green paddy whispers in the
streaking light of the flame-orange sunset. Appearing in silence, the Ruling Party
emerges single-file from a path carved out of the field. Careful not to so much as glance at
the Opposition, they sit down cross-legged, in the shade of the giant tree. Securing his straw hat
on his head, the Speaker of the House places his chair exactly in the middle, nodding in the direction
of the note-takers who hold their pencils poised above their lined exercise books – waiting.

Parliament is in session under a mango tree.

Clearing his throat, the Speaker of the House stands straight as an iron pole, ceremoniously
beginning today's session with a booming announcement. 'Education is the topic of the day,'
he states, half-amused by the sound of his own voice. After a long pause, after he is satisfied
that everyone is listening, he begins again. 'Please proceed,' he says, and the rippling,
grassy field swallows his words whole.

Scrambling to his feet to step into the earthen-clearing, Suresh Kumar, age 9, a
Member of the Opposition, touches the safety pin pretending to be the top-button of his
blue shirt. 'In my opinion, all children in India deserve to get a chance to go to school
and to learn things that they would like to learn.'

Scratch. Rustle. The note-takers begin to scribble.

Shyly turning around, searching for help from his friends, Suresh scans the crowd,
but there is no sign of help yet. Shrugging his shoulders he manages to add in a small
voice: 'I don't think all children go to school.'

Community Cottage School, Dubar Village, Mirzapur District, Uttar Pradesh. CREDA. UNDP. 47

tanding up to smoothen the wrinkles from her blue school uniform skirt, Meera Kumari, age 9, the Education Minister, responds, carefully thinking about every word before she releases it onto the Parliament floor. 'There are schools everywhere and it is the parents' responsibility to send their children there.' Artfully avoiding the Opposition's stares, Meera looks up at the mango tree's stirring leaves. Suddenly a shout cracks into the wide-open field. 'Jhoote! Jhoote! You are not telling the truth!'

Meera

'We have seen how parliament acts on TV and so we act it out here. It is important to know how to ask questions, to know how to change our lives.'

Suresh Kumar, age 9.

Jumping up and down and spinning in circles, the entire Opposition is on its feet protesting.

   'Jhoote!' The shouts come one after another in rapid succession.

   'You are lying!'

   'Tell the truth or sit down!'

   Meera stands her ground, and although she is becoming visibly more embarrassed, even turning slightly red, the Opposition continues to yell. Clenching his fist, Suresh pumps it back and forth, helping to make his point. 'There are villages without schools!' he shouts, full of confidence now that his friends are on his side.

   'Jhoote! Jhoote!' the crowd squeals, excitedly celebrating the noise, and spinning in more circles. Running and jumping into the Opposition, tumbling on the ground as if in the middle of a giant Rugby scrum, a boy yells: 'When there is one teacher and 300 children who wants to go to school?'

Suresh

45

Quickly getting to his feet, the Speaker clears his throat once more. 'Um, hum,' he says for effect, and then in a momentary lull of the explosion, he asks in a calm, official voice if the Opposition would mind sitting quietly. Grinning mischievously, the Opposition grudgingly takes their seats. Still murmuring and threatening, they decide to wait for the next time they can yell again.

'I like shouting the most,' Suresh confides with naughty delight. 'The Ruling Party gives a false statement and we yell when we know they are wrong. Yelling is the best part, that's why I always choose to be on the Opposition. We yell and the Ruling Party just has to sit there.'

Still standing, but wary of the Opposition's ability to explode, Meera begins again twiddling her fingers behind her back: 'We know there are not enough teachers, too many students.'

Kamlesh Kumar, age 9, a Member of the Opposition, stands up slowly. 'Well then what will you do about it?' Kamlesh glances at his friends sitting in the shifting shadows, 'I didn't use to go to school,' and looking back at Meera, he adds, 'Nor did you.' Raising an eyebrow at the fellow members of his Opposition, as if to say, 'Get ready to yell', Kamlesh sits down.

Preparing for battle, Meera tightens her red ribbon and responds swiftly. 'We have opened schools in villages and appointed teachers, but it's up to you, the people, to watch and make it work. We cannot be everywhere.' Standing her ground, Meera watches the Opposition warily. A note-taker scribbles, quickly turning her page. The Opposition rumbles, threatening to explode once more. A few members bounce in the back rows, arms half raised to protest. But this time the President rises. Weighing down the Opposition's bubbling emotions with his open hands, he calmly addresses the Ruling Party. 'A point has been made. Take action to make sure there are schools everywhere and that teachers are teaching interesting things.' Nodding at his own words, the President sits down on his wooden chair, quite pleased with himself.

The Opposition murmurs, the Speaker clears his throat, and the Ruling Party agrees, leaving a vacuum of hushed silence for Meera, relieved, to be able to plop down onto the floor and disappear. Sealing the minutes of the meeting with a stamp, the note-takers assemble their notes and present them to the Speaker.

It's official, The Mango Tree Parliament has concluded for the day. In the scattered light, Seema Kumari, age 10, puts her long arm around Meera's shoulder, whispering as only a friend could. 'When you know that at any moment the crowd will yell, you really have to believe in what you're saying. Otherwise they will just yell and it's all over anyway.'

Still a bit rattled from the exploding shouts of the Opposition, Meera smiles but does not say a word. Finding their backpacks, Seema hands Meera's to her and shrugs: 'Or else you'll just have to yell louder than they do.'

Meera cups a hand over her mouth, giggling at the thought, and the two girls turn arm in arm to follow several rowdy members of the Opposition on their way home through the fluorescent green field.

Being a part of this Children's Parliament gives these a children who belong to a Dalit tribe a chance to stand up for what they believe in. Thousands of children in the carpet belt of UP do not go to school because they have to work in the fields or make carpets. Community schools give children all they need to be able to go to school: school uniforms, pencils and lunch – and when they are up to speed, the kids enroll in government schools.

KARGIL GAMES

Standing on her tiptoes, Kameez Fatima, age 7, reaches up to put a cutout drawing of a smiley face with crayoned, pink cheeks in the paper pocket on the wall. Marking her attendance, Kameez knows that she is 'here', going to school in Kargil.

Government Primary School, Minjig Village, Kargil District, Jammu & Kashmir. Save the Children UK.

Across both India and Pakistan children know that their countries fought a war against each other in Kargil in 1999. Minjig Village, where Kameez goes to school, is 12 km away from Kargil town, very close to the Line of Control between India and Pakistan. Army trucks still scale the surrounding sandstone mountains, and in town they take children to school. But the war brought something else to Minjig village; it brought games to this government school.

'When the war came, we knew we had to do something to get over what hurt so very much,' recalls Ahmed Ali, Kameez's teacher.

Because of the war, parents, teachers and children decided they could not go on with business as usual, reading and memorizing lessons in school. Children needed a place to smile. So, together they started to make learning fun. A village meeting was called and the children were asked what they would like to do. The children had endless ideas.

Many families in Kargil belong to the Shia Muslim community. Women and girls cover their heads, and men and boys attend mosque when prayers echo through the towns and villages over a loudspeaker.

'Now we make our lessons together, the children and me,' Ahmed smiles, buttoning his black leather jacket over a traditional brown kurta.

Now crows, camels and elephants dangle from the ceiling; large rocks are piled in the corner painted with English letters, and still larger rocks boast pictures of things to be spelled, decorated in bright red and green. There are stacks of hand-drawn cards made by the children, and everyone sits on soft, warm, woven rugs.

Tucking her white headscarf behind her ears, Kameez marches over to a circle of kids sitting on the floor in the middle of a chaotic mess of cards. Dotted cards, number cards and picture cards fly through the air. Cards are matched, passed around and found. Mehoub Ali has discovered what he wants to do and is busy building a line of Urdu letters that goes right out of the door. 'In Urdu we go right to left, not left to right like in the English alphabet,' Mehoub explains holding up a card. 'L is for Larki,' he says, turning the card over to show a smiling girl.

Kameez

55

'That's me,' Kameez exclaims, laughing wildly as she falls down on her hands and knees.

During the war, while the children were battling their sadness by playing games, more children kept arriving at their school. Children and their families were moving away from the fighting to safer places like Minjig village. As the games continued, the children of this government school wanted to find a way to build a bridge across to those new children who were so foreign. Mohammed Isaq, age 12, sitting in the classroom next door to where Kameez is playing cards, remembers: 'The children who came to our village came from far away and they were different from us, they spoke another language. It was difficult to get to know them because they were scared and shy and used to stay together in groups of their own. We did not talk to them because we did not know how. Then one day we started playing Kabaddi Kabaddi and someone asked them if they wanted to play, I am not sure who, but they joined in and that day we became friends.' Mohammed smiles shyly. 'We thought people who came from towns were brighter and cleverer than us, but it turned out that we knew just as much as they did, we just knew about different things.'

Moving back and forth across time, Mohammed opens the door to his memories. 'When the war was on we would hear shells drop in the town and would race home from school to stay indoors. We bolted the windows and the doors with latches and big wooden boards until the shelling stopped. We did not go back to school on those days.

↑ Mohammed

56

'We still hear blasts in Kargil town from time to time, so we think the war might come back, but until a shell falls in our village we will stay.' Mohammed looks down at his hands. 'I don't know why people fight.'

In a blur of purple, Kameez rushes past the open door leading a line of girls into the school's garden of waving wild flowers. It's break time. Hopscotch for the girls, and for the boys, today they decide to play a game of Kabaddi Kabaddi – after all, that's what you do when new kids come to school.

Kabaddi Kabaddi

Choose two teams. Draw a large square in the dust and divide it into three. Two teams stand facing each other on either side of the square. The middle zone is safe and the third nearest you is your team's safe zone. Whoever is first starts the game by coming forward saying 'Kabaddi Kabaddi' over and over again, trying not to lose his or her breath. Come as close as you can to the other team's part of the square and then cross over the line. If you are not caught and have not stopped saying 'Kabaddi Kabaddi', then you are safe to return home. But if you lose your breath or are caught, you have to go over to the other side.

Thousand pillar temple is one of the tourist place in warangal. It was built by kakatiyas on 1163 A.D. Every year on 21st February, Shivaratri poojas are done on grand scale.

TEMPLE

We sang lingastastakan in the temple we

WALK

Went round the temple I see cows there

1. 1163A.D by kakliyas
2. We sang lingastakaminthe temple.
3. We went round the temple.
4. There is a holy water outside temple
5. We went to the temple In a auto.
6. We enjoyed in a auto.
7. We saw a cow there

Arriving in a long line of nine yellow auto-rickshaws blasting the James Bond theme music, children in pink uniforms stride past the ancient pillars of stone.

'What do you see? What do you like? What is remarkable to you? Beware, do not try to count the pillars,' their teacher warns, picking up her sari to step inside the temple. 'Legend says those who tried, only managed to get to 999 and then they died.'

'Died?' a voice questions from the crowd.

'So they say,' the teacher smiles. Carefully stepping over the sacred stone entrance that feet should never touch, children weave through this ancient Shiva temple dating back to AD 1163 that like all Shiva temples has a giant Nandi the bull.

'Are there really one thousand pillars?' their teacher asks smiling to herself.

'Where do we begin and where do we end?' asks Ravi Kumar, age 10, a little confused. 'It is impossible to count because each pillar is attached to another,' he says slightly defeated even before he has begun.

'There is no ending, no beginning,' huffs Sana Shabnam, age 8, exasperated with Ravi's question. 'We should not count, Ravi, because we have to believe,' Sana insists, fixing Ravi in her stern stare. 'Perhaps it is the greatness of God but then perhaps it is just a riddle.' Sana sits down on the warm stone stairs to buckle up her shoes, but Ravi is no longer listening; he is running out of the temple yard, tripping over his loose laces to find the rickshaw that brought him here. And then, once everyone is safely in their rickshaws, Ravi, Sana and the rest of the kids buzz back to school to draw what they saw in the temple.

A visit to the Thousand pillared temple, the Aga Khan Foundation, Platinum Jubilee High School, Warangal, Andhra Pradesh.

61

FLOWER

Hritesh

फूलों से ज्ञान - पहचान

पंखुड़ी

पुंकेसर

स्त्रीकेसर

अंखुड़ी

पुष्पासन

फूल की रचना का हल

Getting to the root of the matter in a shadowy village classroom, Hritesh Dube, age 12, squints into his microscope, one eye tightly shut. 'You have to close one eye, but that makes the other one water,' he says dizzily looking up, seeing stars. Rubbing his eyes with scrunched up fists, Hritesh bravely goes back down under for another try. 'It's hard to wink, it hurts my eyes.' Hritesh's voice appears half-muffled as he adjusts the mirror beneath the microscope, trying to catch the natural light. Deciding it's all a bit much, and probably better to see his pink flower with the naked eye, Hritesh plucks his flower from under the observation glass and buries it deep into the pocket of his blue shorts. Abandoning the next step in the experiment, he adds by way of explanation: 'Now we are going outside to see what's in the books.' Racing to collect his backpack, Hritesh joins the end of the long line of kids, shovels on shoulders, books under arms, snaking out of the schoolyard along the village road.

62 Government Middle School, Rani Pipariya Village, Hoshangabad District, Madhya Pradesh. Ekalavya.

Weaving past a cow stamped with pink dots and boasting a pair of giant, striped horns, the long line of kids follows the path through the sloping bushes down to a shallow river. Stooping down to unbuckle their shoes, crossing the river in barefeet, the kids arrive on the other side, where the plants in the books come alive.

Following the steps in their textbooks, the kids scatter across the hillside to collect samples of as many different plants as they can find. 'When we can see we draw what we see,' Hritesh says, dismissing any more questions with a waving hand as he disappears into a leafy green bush.

Cutting across the trail Hritesh left behind, Saurab Dube, age 12, re-adjusts the straps of his rough beige backpack and smacks down his hair, which was being scattered by a gusty breeze. 'When I grow up I will be a flower scientist,' Saurab says, matter-of-factly leading his expedition of three boys on a mission down to the river. Stepping into the realm of social science, Saurab raises his index finger and sums up his vision as if addressing a press conference, 'People like to look at flowers — so I will always have a job.'

Excavation sites set up everywhere, the kids begin investigating the bushes from the inside-out. Getting to the root of things by raising their pickaxes high above their heads, they dig deep into the red-sand-ground, uncovering the different kinds of roots from the soft earth. They have been on similar walks before and so they can tell what the roots are by just looking at the leaves.

'Parallel leaves, fibrous root, mono-cotyledon seed. Horizontal leaves, tape root, dicotyledon seed,' Hritesh reports, sounding like a page ripped out of a botanical glossary. Naming all but one of the spiky, leafy plants, Hritesh straps his specimens onto the back of his pack and rejoins his fellow scientists who are now on the move. Pockets, backpacks and minds full, this flower-power expedition heads back across the river, past the painted cow, past the water pump, arriving back at the school's red-ochre veranda, for a closer consideration of their discoveries.

A discussion begins about what the kids have found. What is good for what? Which plants cure stomach aches, which ones are poisonous, and why do we have to protect the plants we have?

Rohit Kumar, age 11, sits cross-legged between his friends on the school veranda, while his teacher draws specimens the kids might have found on the crumbling blackboard. 'I like doing practical lessons because then I understand how things work. When we do the experiments ourselves we see how plants really grow. No one tells us, we learn on our own. If I just saw it in a book, or if you told me, I am not sure I would remember it as well.' Rohit smiles letting his imagination wander through the forest of his mind. 'I want to be a scientist when I grow up. Not exactly the rocket-type of scientist, but I want to find out more about the stars.'

ractical Lessons

'Learning by doing' is perhaps one of the most exciting ways to learn. In this government school, textbooks developed by an NGO called Ekalavya map out practical lessons and experiments children can do themselves. Hands-on learning in government schools is a great way to be able to deal with large numbers of children, who, when divided into groups, can teach themselves and learn from each other rather than relying on a teacher for constant direction.

Sitting down cross-legged in front of Rohit, Hritesh and his backpack sprout prickly, jungle plants. Carefully unbuckling Hritesh's backpack straps, Rohit removes a sample of a particular wild plant, looks at it and says thoughtfully, 'The environment is our life and we have to know how to save it.' And then raising the wrangling plant high above his head for his teacher and his friends to see, he shouts excitedly, 'What's this?'

Breaking into a loud chatter, the kids decide at once that Hritesh has found something just that little bit different, and they furiously flip the pages of their textbooks trying to find out just what it is.

SCHOOL BUS

DOOR STEP SCHOOL

Slowing down in the left lane of a jam-packed city street, a red and white school bus comes to a complete stop in front of a green park. Turning off the engine, the driver opens his tiffin tin and spreads his lunch across the dashboard. Slowly, one after another, kids pop their heads inside the bus's open door. Continuing to eat his lunch, the driver nods as kids jump up three giant steps, climbing past him to take their seats on the floor. Closing his tiffin tin, the driver opens his newspaper. This bus is not going anywhere, but then it does not need to, because this bus actually is a school. Every afternoon, three steps above the steaming smog-filled traffic of Mumbai, kids go to school here in a bus.

23 children, their names safety-pinned to their shirts on coloured circles of card, peer out of the bus windows at the two trees in the park.

Doorstep School, always on the move, Mumbai. UNICEF.

'What is a tree?' the teacher asks, pointing out of the bus window.

'It's green and brown,' answers Joyti Balagoswari, age 11, pulling her ponytail tight with a pink rubber band.

'Is that all?' the teacher smiles, looking out of the window.

'In the light it is yellow,' Joyti continues, popping her rubber band in her mouth.

'And red,' a little voice peeps out from behind Joyti, it's Ansal, age 5, tugging Joyti's flapping dress to make her turn to see his kaleidoscopic tree growing out of an orange-edged blackboard.

Lakhan Suresh Goasavi, age 11, has a round, smiling face and a small tuft of hair longer than the rest. 'I have never climbed a tree but I would like to give it a try,' Lakhan says pressing his nose onto the bus window to see the two trees in the park. 'If there were more than two, I would, but,' and then softly, steaming the glazed window with the closeness of his breath, he whispers: 'I would not want to hurt them.'

Lakhan lives near a cinema and repairs plastic buckets to survive, but everyday he comes here to go to school. Lakhan loves to read Lot Pot comics, which he buys whenever he has an extra four rupees to spare. Before Lakhan started coming to school he did not know how to read. Now it is his favourite thing to do.

Joyti wanders over to watch Lakhan turn the pages of his cherished comic. Joyti has 10 brothers and sisters and her whole family lives in this park. 'Trees grow by eating well and drinking water,' Joyti explains, her eyes wide as she realizes amazed, how just like a tree she is.

Closing the action-packed pages of his comic, Lakhan pulls his oversized once-white shirt back onto his shoulders and adds thoughtfully, 'We have to worship trees to save them.' He pauses, as if what he has said is reason enough, but then thinking further and deeper, he continues: 'We should make pujas like at purnima when women and girls tie red strings around trees, saying prayers and watering them with clean water.' Getting up to find a purple chalk to give his tree purple-plum fruit, Lakhan looks down at the swirling beeping traffic. 'There is no place left to plant new trees in Mumbai,' he says, drawing a giant plum on his blackboard and holding up his wild, tangled tree with sprouting multi-coloured roots for all to see. 'So we have to look after the ones we have.'

SCHOOL-ON-WHEELS

Mumbai is a very crowded city with very little extra space and the trouble is that everyone wants to live here. After all, this is where dreams come alive on the big screen, this is the home of Bollywood where hundreds of movies are made every year. Apartment buildings climb high into the sky, vying for space with the families who move into this packed metropolis believing life will be better in Mumbai. Once called Bombay, this same city has the highest number of residents per square kilometre in India. So if you want to build anything new, including a new school, finding space is the first problem. But this school in a bus can park anywhere, and so it does, giving the children who live in the park a chance to go to school.

MH·01·H5791

डोअर
स्टेप
स्कूल

lunch

L unch time around India is a multi-cultural celebration:

rice, daal, chapati, subzi, sambar, lemon rice, poories

and parathas — kids around the country eat all kinds

of delicious things, spiced with chilli, flavoured with

lime pickle, sweetened with spices, brought to school

in tiffin tins of all shapes and sizes.

...Where you live,

determines what kind of lunch you enjoy

because it seems

time

day plan

And it's official, the midday meal plan has been passed which means kids in government schools will be given lunch at school. That's great news, because for many kids' families the fact that 'lunch' is given free of cost, is reason enough to send their kids to school.

everyone eats
something just a little bit different everywhere in India...

JACK FRUITS + GIANT ANTHILLS

Walk on the wild side with the Paniya Tribe. Paniyas are wanderers who only collect what they need. Wandering has always been their way of life.

ACCORD, Vidaya Matriculation School, visiting Chembakolly Village, Gudalur Taluk, Niligiri District, Tamil Nadu. Action Aid.

Giant jackfruits hang high in the bark-splintering trees. They are a prickly, yellow-green. Swivelling in the wind, the hard-skinned fruits twist to watch the children weave through the sun-scorched reed-grass far below. Electric purple, dancing turquoise and searing lime green, the children roam in their swaying dresses and worn cotton. These children belong to a tribe, and although they follow their own desires – rubbing lemon grass between thumb and finger to release the sharp scent, allowing giant flame-red ants to scurry over their fingers and thumbs, tasting sweet yellow flowers – they always come back to move together, as one.

Going to school in these red hills means going to school outside; after all, tribal children have grown up wandering with their world. In fact, children from the Paniya tribe are so used to wandering that they used to wander right past the local school that just stood too still, the idea of sitting in a classroom was strange and foreign to them. Like most schools the nearby government school was rooted to the ground, so although the Paniya children paused to look inside, they did not choose to stay. Lessons there are taught in Telegu, which is a foreign language when yours is something else.

'Paniya children speak Paniya,' Geetha explains, agilely sliding down a slope and striding to the front of the tribe. Geetha's sapphire-blue dress shines and her hair, tied in a ponytail with black string, glistens cinnamon and ochre-orange in the harsh sun. Geetha isn't sure how old she is. None of the Paniyas seem to know. Wanderers don't seem to need birthdays.

80

'Elephants do not scare me, they are just hungry, and that's all,' says Ramesh, holding out his piece of dung.

Ramesh

elephant dung →

Marigan, a tribal elder, is leading today's expedition. Wearing a whitewashed cotton t-shirt, a weatherworn dhoti, and carrying his small son on his hip, he reaches out to hold a glistening green Unnichedy leaf in his hand. 'If you get injured when hunting, crush this, make a juice and put it on your wound. If you are brave, you can eat the fruit… but be careful,' Marigan warns, halting the children's advance along the tropical, red-earth path, 'bears like it too because it is so very sweet.' Carefully letting the leaf return to its branch, Marigan leans on his walking stick and proceeds to take the trail behind a giant red anthill that resembles an elderly man, peering at the children through a pair of spectacles perched on the tip of his crooked nose.

Scent of lemon grass

Behind the back of the giant anthill, Rajesh grabs a handful of sharp stems, scrunching and holding them to his nose, 'The sharp grass smells like lemon, see? It's called Pull Thailum, it's good for coughs and body pain.' Rajesh has high cheekbones and round, smiling eyes, but he is more interested in the other kids who are leaning into bushes trying to reach something. 'It costs a lot in the market,' he says, continuing to look over his shoulder. 'But here is it free!' Rajesh spins around, racing to catch up with his friends.

K. Viji →

Whistling green beans

Finding a stick on the ground and reaching high into the bush, Rajesh joins in the game of trying to catch the green beans twirling in the breeze. 'Pumullu Kai,' he says, reciting the local name for the singing bean. 'We don't eat the seeds, but…' says Rajesh putting the bean to his lips and blowing as hard as he can – and an echoing whistle sings.

Touch a blood-red bug

K. Viji falls to the back of the trail, walking slowly as he lets a strange, blood-red insect walk from one hand to the other. 'We have to know these things because if we are sick, we can go to the forest and cure ourselves...I learned this from my father who learned from his father, who learned from his father, like that.' Viji watches the over-sized red insect scurry to the tip of his thumb and fly away. 'Maths and English we can learn anywhere, this we only learn here.' Viji smiles, he lost his insect, but he would have let it go anyway because it belongs in the forest. Viji shrugs, looking ahead to see where Geetha is leading the tribe.

Tribal children often do not go to school because they are not used to sitting in one place. They speak a different language and so are often treated differently when they go to school for the first time. Community schools allow tribal children to learn the languages they need to know to attend government schools.

Taste honey flowers

Walking through the cinnamon-scented bushes, Geetha's sapphire shadow is easy to see – for she walks tall, her back as straight as a tree reaching for the sky. 'It's difficult for us to go to school. Parents need us to help at home, to look after the other children.' Geetha's attention is caught by yellow flowers winking in the bright sunshine. 'Taste them – they are sweet – they have honey in the middle,' Geetha says reaching out to touch… and then adds, wistfully, 'Thottavadi. Touch it – it closes when you do.' Dusting the flower's sweet nectar across her lips, Geetha continues thoughtfully, a word or two for every step: 'I never went to a government school because there you have to sit in one place. There you cannot walk around. There you are not free to move.' Geetha tilts her head back to catch a glimpse of pure-white flowers growing high above on copper-branches. Half-smiling, listening to a Minar bird sing, she says with ease: 'Here we walk. There we cannot.' Placing her tongue on the roof of her mouth, Geetha makes the same clicking sound as the crickets and disappears into the thicket, dissolving into her world. 'This is good for me, here I am free.' And her voice, a slant of turquoise light, is all that is left behind.

83

CHANGING MY S MIDDLE

Raindrops break the lake's glass surface swirling the mountain's reflection into the cold, grey sky. Namaaz prayers echo across the water from a white mosque on the lakeshore and a shikara skims by, carrying two girls, heads covered, on their way to school. Plunging his long paddle into the muddy waters, the shikari moves his shallow boat slowly through

Government Primary School, Moti Muhalla Kalan Village, Dal Lake, Srinagar, Jammu & Kashmir.
Better World, Save the Children UK.

CHOOL IN THE OF A LAKE

the half-submerged barren trees until it stops, hitting ground. Balancing one foot in front of the other, in their practical, heavy shoes, the girls step onto a splintering wooden plank that keeps them just above the sinking mud's reach.

Walking through the drizzling rain, the girls swiftly pass their government school made of wood and stone to disappear behind a high wall. School is closed today, but then schools in Kashmir often are. Teachers go on strike, or simply do not come. The government closes schools when militant attacks shatter towns and villages, and schools are closed on days like today, when religion comes first.

School might be closed today, but there is still a haunting sense of a secret shared.

Follow the girls behind the school and find children, not just one or two, but all of the children who attend this government school, sitting on damp woven rugs in the grey sunshine – there must be over 200 of them gathered here.

On these days when their school is closed, the children call a meeting of their Children's Group for Development (CGD) to discuss, once again, what they can do to improve their school. The children take their group meetings very seriously, making decisions that adults normally make; these children seem much older than twelve or thirteen years old. Although they still live in a world where adults decide their lives, these children have chosen to try to change their world – and it seems they have been doing quite well.

Shabeer Ali, age 12, President of the CGD, wearing a chestnut-brown pheran*, leans forward, his cheeks crimson from the cold, 'We had 200 kids in our primary school and only two teachers.

So we decided to go to the Education Officer on the mainland, to ask for another teacher.

At first he was surprised to see us, but after a minute he smiled and said: "I have never seen children taking up their own issues, you are most welcome."

86

* Pheran, a heavy woolen tunic worn during Kashmir's long winters.

'We sat and talked for one hour'. Shabeer used to be very shy about speaking in front of others; he was embarrassed he did not speak English. But today, confidently, Shabeer tells the children's story in his own language, 'But he didn't give us chai or snacks and that is what is supposed to happen at meetings, isn't it?'

A lot has changed in the children's lives since their first CGD meeting. 'Now children are talking to children about paying attention in lessons. We talk about our problems, which we never did before and we have also started lessons for working children at night...'

Shabeer takes a deep breath and re-arranges the mat beneath him, keeping himself just above the mud. On this island it is difficult for children simply to go to school. 'When something goes wrong schools are closed, teachers don't come and children have nothing to do. Violence has made us all tense. When any of our fathers are out and we hear something has happened we think, when will he be back, one hour, one minute, when? Then there are cases when children lose all of their family in the violence, then what?'

Instilling a calming influence on the meeting, Fatima Battool, age 10, catches the end of Shabeer's conversation, turning the subject back to their school. Fatima's stark-white headscarf seems to light up from the inside against the outside shades of grey. 'We still need more space for our school. We have one room, and it's big, but that's where all the classes go on. We need separate rooms because it's dark in there.'

Afroza

87

Shabeer's face falls back into the streaking shadows as he opens his right hand, counting finger-by-finger the points of their plan. 'There is much more to be done. Right now as soon as you pass out of the primary school you have to cross the lake to go to another school. Girls drop out because their parents don't think it is safe for them to go that far. When it is windy on the lake boats are dangerous for girls because they don't know how to swim. Boys know how to swim, we swim all the time in the summer.'

Gulshan Akhtar's bright green eyes glow from beneath her ivory headscarf. Gulshan, age 12, has not learnt how to swim, but by being part of the CGD she has learned how to suggest plans for changing her school. She raises a hand, leading the discussion onto the subject of quality. 'We still have a problem of making a good school: teachers and students do not arrive on time, both are late and when the teacher talks about moral issues, they help in life, but the other classes,' Gulshan shrugs thinking aloud, 'well, I am not sure how they help.'

Inspired by members from Better World, who suggested that adults were not the only ones who could change their world, these children created their Children's Group for Development (CGD) believing they could make what they learn at school more interesting. Calling their first meeting two years ago, the children raised their hands to elect an executive body of twelve members: eight boys and four girls, including a president, secretary and treasurer – and the CGD has been busy ever since, making changes to turn their school into a place children want to be.

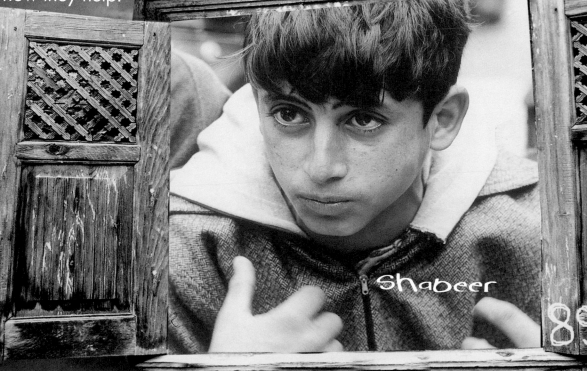

Shabeer

89

Afroza Bano, age 9, rubbing away the takes off her glasses, condensation that has been fogging her view with the edge of her black kameez. Sitting cross-legged, Afroza puts her glasses back on, their tips disappearing into her black headscarf. She smiles with her twinkling, clear brown eyes. 'If they taught us in a better way...'

Gulshan turns Afroza's suggestion over in her mind and thinks aloud, 'If you have two teachers teaching you the same thing, let's say it's nouns – one teacher tells you what it is, and the other uses lots of examples – the second one is the better teacher. That's the one who would make sure children stay in school instead of staying home.'

Shabeer looks strained. There are no easy answers and it's beginning to rain again. Watching the kids roll up their woven rugs to go home, Shabeer ends today's meeting with a question that reveals the struggle he feels inside, 'People don't take what children say seriously. Have you ever found that in the work you do?'

As if reaffirming Shabeer's sentiments, the rain falls more heavily, declaring today's meeting over; until the next time school is closed, until the next time these kids will meet again to discuss once again, how to make their school a place everyone wants to be.

WHERE KIDS TEACH KIDS

Raneeta

Manju

On the roof of Loreto Day School, a bustling private school with 1500 girls, there is another kind of school, a school where girls from the slums come whenever they want to, a school where kids learn from one another, a school named after a rainbow. 'When Rina asks me to teach her, I teach her whatever she wants to know,' says Anwesha Sahwo, age 13, sitting down on the floor in her white Loreto Day School uniform. 'But only when she asks, otherwise we just sit together.'

The Rainbow School, Loreto Day School, Sealdah, Kolkata, West Bengal.

At Rainbow, kids sit in pairs, one from Loreto, one from Rainbow, and help each other through the activities. Kids at Rainbow can do whatever they would like to do. There are many crafts and activities, but if they need help with their homework, they can do that too. All they need to do is ask.

Raneeta Pramanik, age 13, leans over Anwesha's shoulder, wearing her white games kit, ready to run races after class. 'Everyone wants to go to school,' Raneeta says helping Manju Das, age 11, cut bright pink pieces of tissue paper into soft flowers. Sitting against a brightly painted wall of red, yellow and blue, Manju folds the primary colours of a rainbow into blooming petals of her choice. Leaning forward to explain the differences and similarities in the kids' lives, Raneeta continues: 'It's just that some kids have people to help them to go to school and others do not, most times they have to work because there is always a money problem. We have a school with everything, so we can share, we can learn together.' Raneeta looks at Manju for a moment and sums up what she sees. 'I have learned so much from Manju, she made me realize that I live a luxurious life, that I eat so much good food that is so normal for me, food she will never even get to taste.'

Manju smiles, twisting her tissue paper pieces into the petals of a flower. She does not understand Raneeta's story told in English, but she trusts Raneeta to speak for her. 'At Rainbow everything is free, a place to stay, food, uniforms and school supplies. Parents do not have to think about what their kids need, they can just let them come to school. Here there is no difference between kids who live in the slums and private school children. We learn together. Rainbow helps them to be as quick as us, if not quicker, and when they are ready, then enroll in local government schools.' Standing up as the bell rings, Raneeta has one more idea she would like to share. 'All you really have to do is be good friends, if you are friends, then you can ask each other about things that make you nervous or uncomfortable.' Thinking for one more moment Raneeta adds, 'I guess that's the most important thing I have learned, to trust each other, to make sure that both of us are not afraid,' and then, as if Raneeta had been speaking in a universal language all along, Manju holds up her pink flower for Raneeta to take with her to games.

93

BARE FOOT

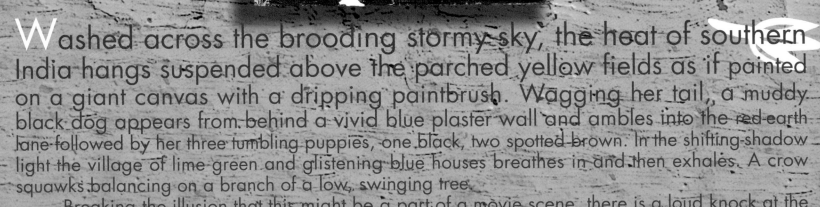

INVESTIGATORS

Washed across the brooding stormy sky, the heat of southern India hangs suspended above the parched yellow fields as if painted on a giant canvas with a dripping paintbrush. Wagging her tail, a muddy black dog appears from behind a vivid blue plaster wall and ambles into the red earth lane followed by her three tumbling puppies, one black, two spotted brown. In the shifting-shadow light the village of lime-green and glistening blue houses breathes in and then exhales. A crow squawks balancing on a branch of a low, swinging tree.

   Breaking the illusion that this might be a part of a movie scene, there is a loud knock at the door. A small, elderly man wearing a dhoti* appears, balancing his bony frame on the frog-green doorframe. Craning his neck to see who has arrived, Kiran, age 9, stands on the doorstep giving him her best full-cheeked smile, 'Hello Putta Tatta*,' she says raising her voice a little louder than she normally would to make sure he can hear what she is saying. Putta Tatta tilts his head inquisitively down and then up. Considering Kiran's blue school uniform, his stern expression dissolves into a grin.

94

'Why are you not in school today?' Putta Tatta asks, flexing his bowed legs to take a step out of his door. Then feeling the heat with his free hand, he changes his mind, deciding it is more comfortable in the shade. 'We are on a survey, Putta Tatta,' Kiran explains, the red ribbons in her hair twisting as she shows him her sheet with drawings of a cow, lizard, cat, goat, dog, elephant, crow and snake. 'Can we ask you?'

* Woven cotton fabric worn by men wrapped around their waists; this finely spun cotton is perfect for keeping cool in the heat.
* Putta Tatta means 'Little Grandfather' in Kannada.

Nalli Kalli, Government Higher Primary School, K. Belthur, Mysore District, Karnataka. DPEP.

95

Leaning on the azure cracked wooden door, Putta Tatta squints to see Kiran's sheet more closely, and then smiling a toothless grin, he nods 'hello' to the other girls. Placing her piece of paper on the mud wall, and holding her pencil almost at the lead's end, Kiran begins the survey. 'What kind of animals do you have in your house?' she asks, staring at her sheet. Putta Tatta smiles, chewing on his lips as most of his teeth are missing. 'Oh, so many,' he says, touching his hand to his head and cackling.

Kiran looks at her friends with a slightly naughty expression. She's not sure how much Putta Tatta is going to be able to help, but he's worth the wait to get an answer. 'So many cows, hens and dogs. We have a large family, that is why we have a lot of animals in our house; every meal we have to feed more than 15 people.' Waving his arms like the village storyteller he is, Putta Tatta makes sure he has all of the children's attention. Kiran marks many cows, hens and dogs on her sheet with lots of little lines. 'What do they eat?' she asks, her finger moving down her list.

Deciding without warning to turn around and end this little chat, Putta Tatta mumbles, 'Whatever they can find.'

Kiran persists, calling after him as he wanders away, 'But Putta Tatta, we have to know what?' As the elderly man's white dhoti disappears into the shadows of the dark village house Kiran and her friends' dusty bare feet trail back to their classroom to evaluate their notes with the help of their teacher.

'What did you find that surprised you?' their teacher asks, sitting down on the floor to be the same level as the kids.

Teja, age 9, sits up on his knees, his eyes wide in the shadows. 'We saw that people live in different houses. Before I had only seen my own house, but now I see there are houses with Bangalore tiles, country tiles, thatched roofs. Some houses were small, some big and some bright blue.'

'And the animals?' their teacher smiles looking down at his list.

Nandeesh, age 9, walks over on his hands and knees pretending to be a cat, 'A grandmother told me that lizards eat mosquitoes and an older man told me snakes eat rats.' And then, stretching like a contented cat who is about to go to sleep, he adds: 'I wish we could go on a survey everyday.'

Their teacher smiles as his kids turn into the animals they have seen. A dog barks, a waddling lizard flicks its tongue. 'Who knew the most? Who could answer your questions?' their teacher persists.

Kiran's hand shoots up in the air, her eyes bright remembering Putta Tatta, 'Grandfathers and grandmothers were able to tell us everything because they are old.' Kiran shrugs, crumpling the pages of her survey in her hands. Watching a shadow move across the sky through the open window she whispers wistfully, as if she is the only one in the world who is watching the rain begin to fall, 'Like Putta Tatta – they have been here forever.'

Walk About
Village surveys give children a chance to find out more about where they live, form questions by themselves and find their own answers. Surveys begin to dissolve the fear that many children have when it comes to asking adults questions.

97

Thursday afternoon in the winding streets of Old Delhi and the traffic is in full swing. Wobbly cycle rickshaws carry passengers on blue-cushioned seats, battling for space with lumbering green buses puffing out grey clouds of smoke. Black and yellow Ambassador Taxis honk, narrowly avoiding collisions with bewildered roaming cows. And as Delhi's street dogs bark, joining in the chaotic scene, black exhaust gushes out, filling the only space left in between.

Somehow every Thursday twelve boys make their way through these chaotic, teeming streets, travelling by foot, bus or borrowed ride, to arrive here – an empty dance room in Presentation Convent School.

Horns fade away into another world as the boys, aged 8 to 16, emerge one by one out of the city that makes its own rules. Wearing baseball hats, faded puffer jackets and jeans held up with strings, large and small, thin and tall, they arrive. The boys come from all over Delhi, but they come for one reason – they are journalists and they have stories to file. They call their newspaper *Wallpaper* because they paste it on the walls of Delhi for everyone to read. *Wallpaper* is a street children's newspaper and all of the reporters are children who live and work on the streets of Delhi.

BREAKING NEWS

BAL MAZDOOR KI AWAZ

EDITORIAL MEETING

Sonu, age 13, the editor, walks through the door zipping up his brown jacket. 'Who has brought interviews today?' Sonu asks, standing above the boys sitting in a circle on the floor. 'Hello!' Raju, age 12, calls out, insisting on an introduction. Sonu laughs, flopping down on the floor. The meeting has begun.

Wallpaper reporters are used to starting conversations by asking questions first; they often have to be the first to walk up to street kids they have never met and interview them about their lives. A *Wallpaper* reporter has to be kind, sensitive and sincere to get his story – and they all are, because they know exactly how it feels to live on the streets of Delhi. They live there too.

Parvez, age 12, raises his hand, he wants to report. 'Give a clap for Parvez,' Sonu yells. The boys clap wildly and a slightly embarrassed Parvez unrolls a piece of paper he has scrunched up in his warm hands. 'I interviewed Mehbuk who lives in the railway station where I live.' Looking down at his page torn out of a wide-lined notebook, Parvez carefully reads aloud in Hindi:

'My name is Mehbuk. I am a rag picker and I live in Fatehpur Station in Old Delhi. When I go ragpicking the cops stop me and check my stuff. They take any iron or steel item and then they beat me because they think I have stolen it. The man who I sell to always gives me 1 kg less than what it is actually worth. Then when I do have money, and go to buy something for myself, he shoos me away saying I am a thief.'

Sonu

Dance Room,
Presentation Convent School,
Chandni Chowk, Old Delhi.
Butterflies.

99

Sonu leans forward intrigued: this is 'news'. 'Can you find out more? Who are the cops that beat him? Who pays him less? Our job as reporters is to find out as much as we can so we can help change the situation.'

Parvez looks at his article, rolls it up and puts it into his pocket.

'No, we need it! It's good,' Sonu laughs, patting him on the back.

Street Children

Many children become street children because they have been mistreated in some way: beaten at home or school, overworked, abused, or their families are simply too poor to take care of them. They leave home in search of a better life. When children run away they often sneak onto a train that is going to a big city like Delhi, arriving to work and live on the streets, finding odd jobs they can do to survive. Some boys become chai boys who deliver tea in glasses, others work cleaning tables and washing dishes in restaurants, and yet others go rag picking, collecting rubbish that can be sold.

But a large number stay on the railway station platforms where they first arrived, refilling mineral water bottles from a tap to sell and shining shoes.

Street children can make enough to survive by working on the streets, but most of them never go to school again. Many children live in the overnight waiting rooms at railway stations where a bed for one night costs Rs 3*. NGOs like Butterflies work with street children so that they always have a place to go to if they need help. To survive on the streets of a big city means you have to be very tough and very smart. Although street children do not go to school, they learn in other ways; the streets are their school. Writing a newspaper such as *Wallpaper* gives the kids a chance to express themselves.

*Rs 45 = Approximately 1 US$

Turning bright red, Parvez hands over his crumpled report and Sonu is on to the next one. 'Javed?'

Javed, age 13, is next, but he has not interviewed any children. Sonu raises an eyebrow, 'What should happen to you since you failed to bring a report?'

'Why are you asking me?' Javed replies, amazed he has been asked such a question.

'As this is a democratic set up, you can decide how you will be punished,' Sonu points out, sounding like a politician.

'Sing a song from any film that lasts five minutes,' Anuj pipes up.

Javed shakes his head and is saved from singing by Afroz, age 9, who whispers, very quietly, as he looks down at his hands: 'I don't have a report because I lost my pencil.'

Sonu changes from a witty editor into a kind friend, and leans in to whisper: 'Don't worry, we will find you another one.'

Afroz will not look up from his hands.

A small knock at the door and a chai boy* arrives in the room, his left hand flowering with white, ceramic teacups.

'Tea Time!' Sonu announces as the little chai boy hands out packets of biscuits that are opened and crunched. This is the best part of the meeting. Javed turns his blue baseball cap backwards and considers, as he dips his biscuit in his steaming chai, why they bring out their newspaper. 'A minister gets a fever, it is on the front page, a child dies and no one cares.'

Javed blows on his hot chai to cool it and looks into his teacup. It is not easy to live on the streets of Delhi. Sometimes it is even harder to talk or write about it. When Javed writes for his newspaper he is writing about his life. The interviews he collects from other children could be his own. Javed sinks his biscuit even further into his teacup and continues:

* Boys who work delivering chai – tea boiled with milk, sugar and spices.

101

'**W**e bring out this newspaper because we want to show adults...even those who shun us and refuse to speak to us... that being poor will not stop us from telling the world our problems.' Sonu, age 12

'Children's problems are neglected. We have a lot of children living on the streets, they have so many problems, they get beaten up and they are sick all the time – if we don't write about it no one will know.' Javed looks up at the ceiling and turns his baseball cap around the right way. When Javed is not on a *Wallpaper* assignment, he collects plastic teacups at the Old Delhi railway station, and depending on how many he collects, he can sell them for up to Rs 50. Javed works in the morning and then hangs out with his friends. He has been collecting teacups for three years. Coming over to give the chai boy back his cup, Javed says in a very grown-up way: 'We all have dreams – but who knows what will really happen.'

The little chai boy shifts uneasily from foot to foot. His sneakers are too big for his feet and the laces trail behind him on the floor.

Sonu follows the little boy's stare, asking him his name and what his dreams are. Shyly burying his face in his hands, and peeking once more at Javed, the boy stays silent. He cannot answer. Sonu concentrates on this fellow street child and finds an end to his story so it can be sent to press, 'Perhaps he dreams of becoming a journalist on *Wallpaper* just like Javed.'

Javed is busy drawing a picture of a chai boy for the next edition of their newspaper.

'Or maybe he just wants to wear a blue baseball cap backwards... that would be just like Javed too.' Sonu eases back onto his brown-socked heels to see a handful of white teacups, now stained with tea, swinging out of the door into the teeming streets from which he, and all of these boys, came.

500,000 children live on the streets of India. 12 of them have a newspaper to say how they feel.

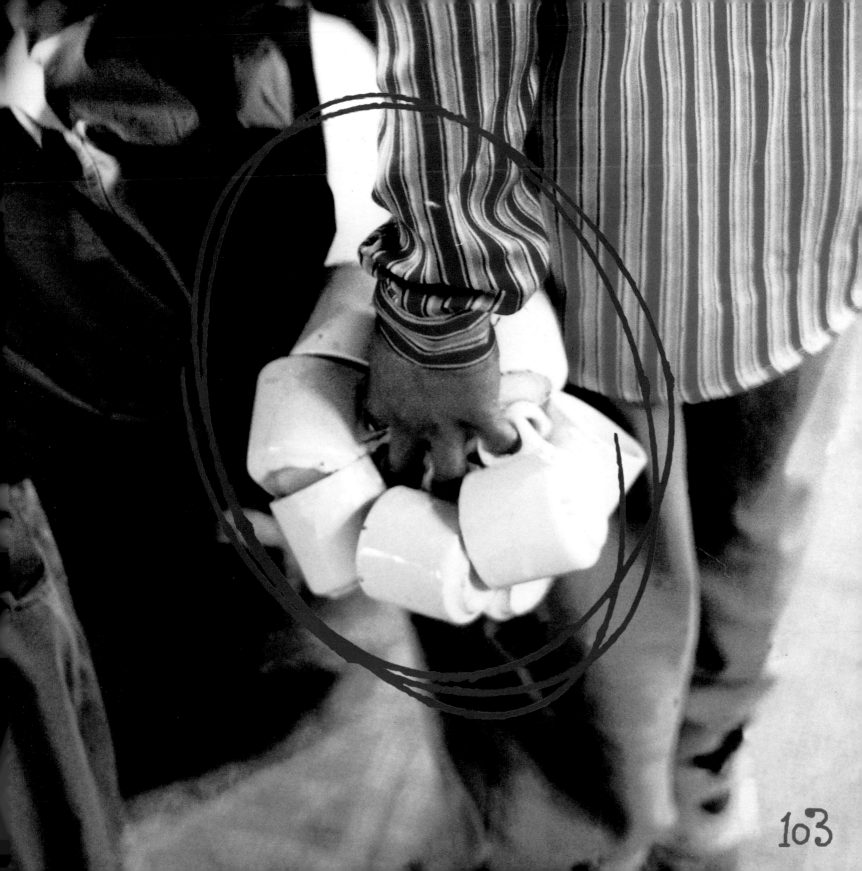

103

BACKWATER EXPERIMENTS

Glass bottles of all sizes wait silently on wooden desks in a shadowy-dark classroom; some are tall and thin, others are clear-blue and some are very small. The early morning light reveals names pasted on the bottles in hand-written, squiggly Malayalam: Vidya, Shivraj. When seen on a page Mallayalam is a language that loops and winds in a continuous flow, just like the interlocking, curving waterways for which Kerala is so well known.

Opening the classroom window, the teacher pauses for a moment to watch a large red boat motoring through the trees. Turning around to begin, she adjusts her thick glasses more comfortably on her nose, flips her long braided hair over one shoulder and picks up a bottle filled with murky water. Holding it up to the light she considers it sceptically. 'Do you think the water in your bottles is clean?'

Government LPS Mankampu, Pullinkunnu Village, Alleppey District, Kerala. BGVS.

Zooming in on their bottles to take a closer look, eyes swelling, magnified by the glass, the kids look like giant blinking insects awakening from a long nap.

Vidya S. Kumar, age 9, has two pony tails that swing from side to side as she looks up wide-eyed from her water-sample. 'Yes, it must be, we drink it so it has to be clean.'

The teacher smiles, smoothening her blueprinted sari over her shoulder: 'Well, let's see.' Lifting a finger as if leading an expedition to one of the poles, she says in a directorial way: 'To test your water, you will need: one, a magnifying glass to notice the small things; two, a flashlight to shine light on the bottle of water; and three, a white card to place behind the bottle.' Softening her stern expression, she adds mischievously, 'You are lucky, for today we have all of those things.' Three by three the children approach their teacher's desk to test their water in the light.

'What can you see?' the teacher asks.

In Kerala's backwaters, a series of interlocking water lanes, water is a way of life. Water threads in and out of the land and the children's lives, and so it's essential that the water the children drink and the water they travel through remains clean. Pollution is clogging many of the water lanes with weeds and polluting the ground water which feeds the pumps that provide the water children drink.

105

'Small creatures are swimming,' answers Vidya, her nose pressed to the magnifying glass. 'Ugh! There are bugs in the water,' she exclaims jiggling the bottle. 'Shake the water again – see the bugs!'

Clinking their bottles together, the kids compare their samples, amazed the water they drink is not as clean as they thought. Their teacher squeaks her wooden chair across the wooden floor, pulling herself closer to her desk, 'Where do you get the water you drink?'

Raising his hand, Shivraj Shankar, age 9, holds a particularly muddy bottle of water between his two small, grimy hands, 'I got this water from the river. Every morning I have a bath in it and after school I play cricket by the river. This is the water I drink,' he shrugs, wearing a smudged beige t-shirt that is not part of the school uniform. 'I guess it's not so good.'

The teacher looks at him with her first real, full smile. 'No, Shivraj, I guess not. How could you keep your water clean?'

Shivraj smoothes his sticky hair down with his right hand and looks up at his teacher with big eyes. He is not sure what to say. As he pauses hands shoot up in the air competing for attention. Choose me, they seem to say, choose me. And the teacher does, one by one.

Shyam A. Kannan, age 9, very proud that he has been chosen first, takes a deep breath. 'First we will put a net on the top of the wells so there is no bathing or washing in the well, then we will build a separate wall to keep the cows away.'

Aparna Soman, age 9, sitting in the window, holds her small, clear bottle against the light, 'When people wash and bathe around the hand-pump the dirty water gets inside. That makes you sick with amoebas and diarrhoea.'

Sreeranj S. Kumar, age 9, sitting forward on the edge of his bench, wants to launch a campaign. 'I will draw pictures of women collecting water and put posters around town that say, 'only take pure water' and 'don't pollute'. My mother carries water from the well and she boils it before I drink it, so she is the one who keeps it clean. Mothers look after water the most, you have to talk to them.'

'Fathers too,' adds Shivraj of muddy t-shirt fame, hiding behind his teacher's sari. Shivraj's mother died last year, so for him this campaign would need to be changed a little bit. Shivraj's once stern teacher turns around to place her strong hands on both of his shoulders. posters would you make?'
Shivraj shrugs, concentrating; he dumps his bottle upside-down, right side up, and then shakes it once again, 'I'd make them for farmers so they can learn to take care of the water – because when I am bigger I will grow paddy like my father.'

Bending down to catch Shivraj's gaze the teacher smiles, but Shivraj is only interested in his murky bottle. 'Fathers that are farmers,' she says, finding the link between work, family and water.
'Hmmmm,' Shivraj hums, using both of his small hands to clink his large cloudy bottle carefully down on his wooden desk.

Shivraj

107

BANANA SPLIT

In the back alleyway of steamy Bangalore there is a mini-government school built like a train. Two rectangular carriages, or rather, classrooms, wait in silence for midday exams to end. Arriving in groups of two or three, children who have finished their exams early slip off their shoes at the classroom door and scatter across the stone floor. Beneath the children's feet the floor is so highly polished that when they tilt their heads to see, their expressions, noses, searching eyes and grins stare back at them, asking when they will look away and start to play. A bell rings in the classroom next door. Exams now over, the fun can begin.

Government Lower Primary School, Kannada Medium, JP Nagar Slum, Bangalore. Suvidya.

Two teams. Two sides. The children line up barefoot in an excited, hushed silence. Guru Prasad, age 11, walks past, his long lanky legs and bony knees popping out of his short blue shorts, as he gives each contestant a number. '1, 7, 9, 2, 4, 12,' he says with a quirky grin, placing his hand on the newly numbered shoulders.

The numbers stay silent, memorizing their new identities. Standing on their tiptoes, holding their breaths, they wait and watch as Guru bends down, his fingers white with chalk dust, drawing a circle in the middle of the shiny floor. Placing one small banana that looks like a gorilla finger in the centre of the circle, he takes four giant steps backwards towards the blackboard and scribbles numbers as largely as he can.

2 X 6.

And then like a ringmaster at the opening night of a circus, he asks in a lifting voice, his face breaking into a giant smile: 'What is two times six?'

Tussle, scuffle, the 12s race out, skidding on the floor. Numbers and audience scream, cheering on their team. Who will be the first to grab the banana? The team who wins the most points will win the bananas. The Numbers squeal. So it seems you can help your team by screaming the most and the loudest.

Several rounds later, Murli, age 9, a member of the winning team, grins as he peels his prize monkey style. 'We are so proud of winning that it does not feel like maths,' he shouts, his mouth full of banana, and little banana chunks sail through the air.

Guru tugs at his shirt, reminding him not to talk with his mouth full, but Murli pulls away fighting through the excited crowd to finish what he wants to say. 'When we play we forget it's school.' Murli the Banana King has started a trend – now everyone wants to yell about how important maths and bananas are. Hands shoot up, fighting for attention.

'I buy rice for my mother so I have to know how much half a kilo and one kilo are, how much they cost and how much change I need,' says Muttoo, age 10, crawling out of the riotous crowd on her hands and knees. A worried expression darts across Muttoo's gaze as her index finger darts up to see if the small gold ring is still clinging to the side of her nose. She smiles relieved, it is.

'You've got to know how to count green coconuts too,' says Ravi, age 11, bending down to help Muttoo to her feet. 'My father goes to buy coconuts from the wholesale market and then he sells them.'

'Only bananas!' yells Satya, age 10, pushing away Guru who is trying to keep some kind of order but failing miserably. 'My neighbor sells bananas – you need to know how much those are too.'

'Naar just eat them!' Murli yells, mouth still full of banana, and his yell sets the classroom on fire. Kids erupt like popcorn popping, cackling, screaming and skidding across the floor. Guru raises his eyebrows, realizing the only way to regain control is to bend down again and draw another circle. His plan works. Noticing that Guru is beginning the next round, the numbers scramble back into their lines, telling each other to be quiet until they can once again scream for more.

111

PUPPET SHOW

Under a tree on a railway platform, 27 children sit in a semi-circle singing about peacocks. It is 8 a.m. Trains pull into the station blowing their whistles, but the children do not seem to notice. A teacher wrapped in a bright green sari, her black hair parted perfectly down the centre, carries a large tin box out onto the platform. Catching their breath, the children watch quietly as their teacher awakens the puppets from their stainless steel box. All of the children who go to school here live and work on the railway platform.

Two barefoot girls jump up, offering to hold the patterned cloth. Ensammee, age 6, dips his hand into the open magic box, stacking Oriya flash cards in different shaped piles on the cement floor, and Amla, age 9, a small girl named after the green-yellow crab-apple fruit, spins a globe on the platform, watching the world move through her tangled hair. A train whistle blows once more and, putting their fingers in their ears, the children watch as the curtain goes up and the show begins.

112 Ruchika Social Service Organization. Platform School, Bhubaneswar Railway Station, Bhubaneswar, Orissa.

The orange-puppet-teacher with large, drawn coal black eyes pops up behind the material stage. 'Wash your hands!' she shouts to the yellow puppet with diarrhoea who has not been washing his hands after going to the toilet.

Feeling very sick, the yellow puppet groans loudly. Struggling with a stainless steel cup too big for her, a newly arrived pink puppet assumes the voice of a doctor. 'Drink this each time you have a tummy ache,' the puppet exclaims, swinging the cup from side to side. 'Just mix water, sugar and salt, but don't make it saltier than your tears!' Humming happily as she mixes the concoction, the pink puppet spills most of the mixture over the side, making the children clap their hands over their mouths in excitement. Even the passengers waiting for their train can't help but chuckle.

Arranging her dusty crimson dress carefully around her, Amla sits up on her knees to watch the puppet show. 'The puppets tell me things I do not know,' she says glancing at her hands, and then hiding them beneath her. Amla's hands are cracked from the work she does. 'That's why I come to school, to see them,' Amla says raising herself up to be as tall as she can be – staring wide-eyed, she searches to see if there might be more left of the show. 'I used to collect things from when the sun got up to until it went away. I collected plastic bags and sold them to the man who has a shop. Now I bring my rag-collecting bag with me to school so I can start collecting when school is finished. Because I come to school I get less money, but no one seems to worry because I am learning things.' Taking one last look at the material stage, Amla lets her breath go as the puppets must go back to sleep in their box for today.

Dissolving into her own world, Amla takes her time placing one bare-foot exactly in front of the other, balancing along the edge of the platform. 'When I grow up I would like to be a dancer,' she whispers as the small, silver bells on the bracelets around her ankles tinkle and she stoops down to pick up a plastic bag someone else has thrown away.

latform Schools give children all they need to come to school: lunches, baths on Saturdays, books, chalks, slates and medical care when they are not feeling very well. Lessons in this Platform School focus on what the children need to know to survive and improve their lives. Puppet shows like these help children to understand the world around them. Puppets talk about train routes, post offices, police stations, who to speak to when they need help, opening bank accounts, the sicknesses you can get from unclean water, and the importance of saving money.

Saturday is bath day at the Platform School, when everyone comes to school just to take a bath.

BONES

Once a week, in a hands-on biology class in a Delhi slum, bones are scattered on a blackboard and brought back to life. According to the boys who know this skeleton well, it's much more than just a bag of bones.

'We call him Khushi Lal, because he is a happy guy,' explains Mahinder Singh, age 11, assembling Khushi's cracked skull. Mahinder is leading today's operation and he takes his job very seriously. 'Lift the head, put the jaw underneath,' Mahinder advises, as the boys fall on their knees, kneeling around the bones.

Bones click when the boys find where they need to go, bringing Khushi back to life. And while fiddling with various vertebrae, Aslam Ali, age 11, offers to tell the skeleton's story, 'He was 43 years old when he died crossing the road. The doctor gave him to us and his head was broken. We call him Manoj.'

'His name is Khushi Lal, happy man!' objects Mahinder, lifting the skeleton's skull high above his own in protest.

Aslam gently helps Mahinder put the skull back onto the body. 'He can be whoever you want him to be.'

Suraj

Aslam

Mahinder

Khushi Lal

Searching for Khushi Lal, Mahinder looks inside the skull, 'You use your brain to think, remember and control your body. If we did not have a brain we would be wandering around like madmen.'

Aslam laughs. 'Khushi does'nt have a brain.'

Mahinder ignores Aslam, preferring to imagine Khushi's thoughts. 'Khushi is thinking he wants to live like we do. I dream of becoming a great man and making my parents happy.' Tenderly putting Khushi's skull back together, Mahinder shoots Aslam a sneaky smile. 'He knows what is happening to me will happen to you.'

With Aslam silenced, Mahinder continues with the re-assembly of the man who once was. 'Which bones can we not live without?'

Suraj Kumar, age 12, pulls a face as he points from a safe distance. 'I feel a bit yuk touching the bones,' he says, breathing heavily and waving his index finger high above Khushi's back. 'But we need our spinal column, otherwise we couldn't stand up and the bones that protect our lungs and our hearts are very important too. Some of the skeleton's bones are missing. I guess they broke in the accident. We should really get him an arm and a leg from a hospital.'

Sitting back on his heels, Suraj thinks aloud: 'I wouldn't mind being a skeleton in a school.'

Aslam laughs, being naughty again. 'He never had any teeth.'

As the boys consider Khushi Lal's fate, Amardeep Chauhan, age 12, who has been staring wide-eyed at the skeleton for the entire lesson, speaks: 'Sometimes I feel scared I will become like him.'

'Don't worry,' Suraj responds. 'When he died his soul flew to God.' Aslam shrugs, trying to reassure Amardeep. 'Then he was immediately born into another body.'

Amardeep stares at the skeleton, clearly not convinced.

Changing the subject, Mahinder walks up behind Amardeep and places his hands on his shoulders. 'Come on, let's get our photo taken with the skull.'

Forgetting his worries, Amardeep shuffles forward on his knees, carefully choosing the bones he wants to make famous in the photograph. 'We can make a skull with crossed bones,' Mahinder calls, holding out the skull before him, as he leads a procession of boys into the bright morning sun.

Katha Public School, Govindpuri Slum, Delhi.

117

CHILD RIGHTS

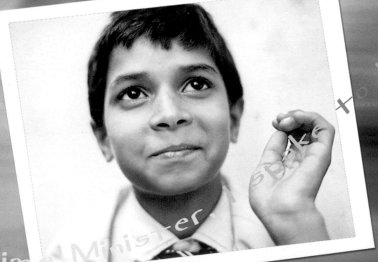

'Dear Prime Minister... to 120 children

Choose a child right, any child right, from the right to go to school to the right to have enough to eat, from the right to say what you think to the right to practice your own religion. Then think for a moment: are children in India receiving their rights? Every year kids across the eastern state of Bihar devise projects to find out if child rights are alive and well in their state – they go from house to house talking kid to kid to find out what's happening. And at the end of the year, they travel here, to the Child Rights Congress, to present what they discovered – in posters, drawings and models; to see who will go home with a prize.

UNICEF Patna, Child Rights Congress, Sitamarhi, Bihar.

CONGRESS

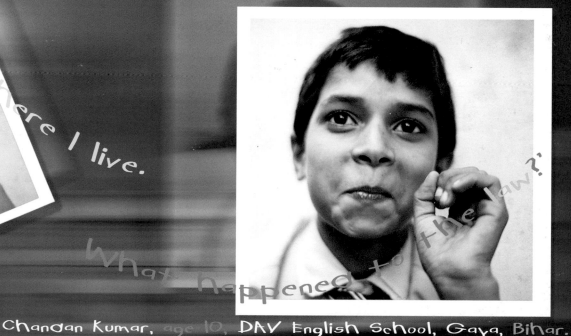

who work where I live.

What happened to the law?

Chandan Kumar, age 10, DAV English School, Gaya, Bihar.

What are child rights? Child rights are what children need to survive and live a healthy life. Every child has the right to have a name, to go to school, to be treated the same as everyone else, to have an opinion, to be protected from harm and to participate in decisions that affect his or her life. You can find out more about your rights by reading The Convention on the Rights of the Child (CRC), a list of over 50 rights that all children should have. Almost every country in the world has signed the CRC, making it the most widely ratified (agreed upon) convention in the world. In 1992, India signed the CRC, taking steps to make children's rights come true.

Child Labour is breaking the law

Sukpur village, Supaul District, Bihar

Krishanand Singh, age 11, pulls his blue baseball hat snugly down on his head. 'Why do some children have to work and others don't?' he asks, placing both hands firmly on the table. 'That was the question we started with and we went house-to-house interviewing kids. In one village where the parents were sweepers, 25 out of 28 children who were old enough to go to school, were working...It made me think that parents of working children have most probably been child labourers themselves. Those parents are afraid, they have no confidence in themselves, they want to know they will always eat and they know that if their children work, they will always eat.'

Alok Kumar, age 11, listens as he arranges the paper flowers they made in a papier-mâché vase decorated with a photo of a cricket player. He then adds, 'Those parents do not believe that school is any good; they don't think it will lead to a job. The government has to make them believe, to find a way to reach them, to talk to them through feelings, moods, plays and songs, to make them understand that going to school is the only way their children's lives will change.'

Krishanand and Alok made over 100 paper flowers and sold them to buy slates and chalk and open a learning centre for working children in their village.

Krishanand

paper flowers

Alok

Girls and Boys have the right to be treated the same

Uma Devi Girls' School, Katihar District, Bihar

Ankila Rani, age 11, rolls out her yellow, scroll paper poster, 'I did not start out wanting to do a project on girls. But when I started visiting houses, I saw that girls were always being treated differently and it made me think... How can I be a girl doing a project on child rights when all of these girls cannot even leave the house? So I changed my project. I made it on girls because girls get less clothes, food, they don't go to school, and the way people behave towards them is just not as good as boys.' Ankila looks down at her poster and decides to make it lie straight on the table. 'I think it boils down to the parents who think their boys will grow up and look after them and girls will leave the house when they get married so any investment in a girl will be lost... But girls can do just what boys can do. We can grow up to look after our parents too, but we need to go to school to be able to do that and if you don't send us, well then yes, you are right, we won't be able to do anything.'

Ankila

An Open Letter to the State Minister of Education

Dear Sir, our school has been occupied by the police and this has ruined education in our village, therefore I request you to take this police camp out of the village as soon as possible, or at least make another building available for the school.

Rakesh

'And I will give him my address and send it with all the children's signatures so we can talk. I will tell him that this goes against Article 28 of The Convention on the Rights of the Child, which is every child's right to go to school and that India signed that.' Rakesh Kumar, age 12, Sahartorari, Bhojpur District, Bihar.

122.

Teach with your heart

SS Girls' High School, Babua, Kimur District, Bihar

Gazala Firdauz, age 11, wears her hair slightly parted off centre, but everything else about her is seriously straight. Gazala is the only one of her project group of four girls who was allowed to travel to the Congress. Acknowledging that girls are often treated differently from boys, Gazala nods, but that's what investigating child rights is all about, talking about things that are normally not discussed. 'I felt school was important for every child so I went to a village to see who really was going to the primary school which was two kilometres away.' Shifting her weight from side to side, she is visibly uncomfortable with what she found: 'Most of the children I spoke to wanted to go to school, it was the adults who were taking children's rights away by saying they had to work...Before this survey, I thought adults were children's friends. I guess not always. Parents make children's rights come true, but then sometimes they don't want to. And when teachers think what they do is only a job, they don't teach with their hearts.' Gazala takes a breath and ends her presentation, 'You've got to use your heart, otherwise no matter what you do it doesn't matter at all.'

Gazala

123

FISHING FOR FACTS

124

IN PONDICHERRY

Hand in hand, jasmine twined in their black-braided hair, a line of girls moves through the cobblestone streets of the old town of Pondicherry.

Past sun-bleached yellow villas of stone; past a woman selling pale pink lotus flowers in the shade; past a policeman with white gloves directing them across the road, the girls stride, setting the scent of coconut oil free in the ocean breeze. White caps on to protect them from the sun, their bright green uniforms glistening as they walk past the temple where a painted elephant lives, the girls walk down to the beach for a science class on the beach.

Today these girls are investigating what it would be like to be a fisherman who lives by the sea. And rather than sit in the classroom, peering at their textbooks, the girls decided to go to the source and interview those who know – the fishermen themselves.

Divided into five groups, today the girls are reporting live. Shanmuga, age 12, is a Fish reporter. Pushing her white cap up onto her forehead so she can better see Kumar, a fisherman, she chews on the end of her pencil. 'What do you do before you go to sea?'

Kumar's skin is tanned black-brown from days in the sun and he wears a worn dhoti wrapped around his waist. Smiling at the girls' official school white socks and shoes sinking into the sand, he answers: 'I was in the sea for the whole day, there is no before, no after, only sea.' Standing barefoot in the scorching sand, Kumar unravels his giant net, letting it fall in fluid layers at his feet.

125

Shanmuga squints into the harsh light: 'Where did you learn to fish?'

'I learned to fish by fishing with my father who learned from his father, who learned from his,' Kumar answers matter-of-factly.

Shanmuga scribbles quickly. 'Will your children learn how to fish?'

Kumar eases a sticky silver fish out of his net. 'It depends how much they learn at school, whether or not they get a job; if not, they will come to the sea with me.'

Shanmuga scrunches up her nose, 'When you are in the middle of the sea, how do you know where you are?'

Kumar chuckles, shaking his head and Shanmuga chuckles right back at him, pulling her hat down to shade her eyes, brave enough now to ask another question she did not write down before: 'Are you afraid of the moon? People say fishermen are afraid of the moon.'

Kumar smiles again. 'How can we be afraid of the moon when she brings the waves? We are all children of the sea and that includes you too.'

Shanmuga closes her notebook, smiling at her newly found friend.

126

Calling all of the girls together, Malani, age 12, a Plant reporter, rests a foot on a heavy wooden kayak that has been carved out of a single giant log. Finished scouring the seashore, the reporters sit down in the sand to share what they found. Malani begins with a query. 'The fishermen say there are blue and yellow flowers under the sea that creepers are attached to rocks and flowers live in the salt water. How can that be? How can flowers grow in salt water?'

Striped Surgeon Fish
(Acanthurus lineatus) × ⅓

Bala, age 13, a Shell reporter, opens the textbook they brought along for this reason. 'It can be true, see here, the book has blue flowers that grow in the sea.'

Sitting on the edge of the kayak, Abirami, age 13, a Fisherman's Life reporter, holds her white cap between her hands and carefully considers what she has found. 'Many boys go to the sea when they are small and keep going until they are eighty or until they die. Most of them only go to school until they are eight or nine.' Abirami glances up at the fishermen, who have come to listen to her filing her report, 'A fisherman said to me: "It's good that you come here for projects, away from school. Now you know how we live, so when you become leaders you won't allow foreign ships to come because they take all the fish, their nets go deeper and their boats go further out to sea."' Abirami pauses, calculating what this means in her life, 'Local fishermen need to be given a chance, but how do you do that? I have come to the seaside so many times with my parents, but I did not know… when we come here to study we see more. We see how hard their lives are.'

127

Angler Fish
(*Antennarius hispidus*) × ½

Listening to the other girls, Kumanuvalli, age 13, an Imagination reporter, swirls a circular pattern in the sand with her index finger. Looking up, she offers what she has imagined, inspired by what she has seen and heard. 'I imagined fishermen must sing songs when they are afraid. Fishermen have an amazing collection of local songs, but when we asked them to tell us they just shrugged. Most of them cannot read or write, but we know they tell poems about life on the sea to each other.' Kumanuvalli watches her friends empty their shoes of sand and remove their socks, sticky with salt water. Unbuckling the buckles of her black shoes, Kumanuvalli finds an end to her story, 'Perhaps they did not tell me because I am not a fisherman. They all belong to a fisherman caste and one man said: "We go to all kinds of temples, we are Hindu, we are Muslim, but it does not matter because we are all fishermen." But even so, I am not a fisherman, so perhaps their songs are their secret.'

Sneaking up behind Kumanuvalli, Kalaishanthi, age 12, puts her hands on her friend's shoulders: 'It should not matter what religion anyone is because we all have to save the sea. Along each part of the sea people are living, our land, wherever we live in the world is next to water, our part of the water is the Bay of Bengal, that is why we have to save the sea here. It's ours.' Kumanuvalli nods as she sets her purple Imagination notebook down, takes her white socks off and flings them into the sand, and grabs Kalaishanthi's hand to pull her into the sea. Tumbling in the waves, the girls squeal, soaking their school uniforms.

'Why is the sea salty?'
Bhanupriya, age 13.

Blue-ring Angel Fish (adult)
(*Pomacanthodes annularis*)   × ¼

A small, white tent sits on the horizon. The playful wind twists the tent's red flag and the endless, cracked mud desert melts as mirages hover under the electric blue sky.

উজাস

GOING TO SCHOOL IN A MIRAGE

Ujas Tent School, Little Rann of Kutchh, Surendranagar, Gujarat. Ganatar. CRY.

A boy rides out of the mirage, the click, click of his bicycle breaking the silence. Anji, age 9, walks barefoot through the desert, her green lehenga* swaying as she moves. Arriving swiftly at the tent, Anji lifts the flap and disappears inside. Smudged with dust, her hair matted into tiny plaits, Anji sits down tracing the contours of the word Welcome, carved into the smooth mud floor. Anji is as silent as the desert.

'Anji is deaf and cannot talk. But nobody teases her here,' Munna, age 11, her brother, explains as he watches her. 'Anji likes coming to school. She plays and writes down everything on the board – she gets very upset if I leave her at home.'

* Lehenga, a full flowing skirt gathered at the waist

132 Anji

Munna follows Anji's stare as she tilts her head to look up at something above her head. Munna sees what Anji sees: a ceiling fluttering with lime green, pink and blue paper flags – orange tissue-paper lanterns dancing in the slight breeze. Munna sees their school: a tent, glowing like a light bulb in the desert light.

A mud desert in the Little Rann of Kutchh* is perhaps one of the last places in the world you would expect to find a school. Here there are no trees, no animals and no birds, but there are children going to school. The water beneath the ground is saline, so sweet water has to be delivered by Chackras – multi-coloured Enfield motorcycles that pull painted wheelie contraptions behind them. Chackra drivers deliver water free of cost to the tent schools because they know how important it is for children to go to school

Every year, the June monsoon turns this desert of 12,000 square kilometres into sea. Water levels rise as high as five feet (taller than Anji or any of the children in this tent). When the rain ends, the water seeps slowly into the ground, leaving salt behind. From November until May, saltpan workers and their families move 25 km or further into the mud desert to make salt. They build houses and install pumps to bring salty water from under the ground into surface basins; water that will crystallize into millions of tiny six-sided salt cubes. Children move into the desert with their families and many would stop going to school if it were not for a tent school nearby.

* Rann, a name for an arid, dry place.

Munna

133

n a blue, plastic tray that holds this precious water, one by one the children blow little drops of oil paint into delicate designs. Anji dips a slice of paper, admires her creation and carefully carries her masterpiece out into the desert to dry.

Just as there is no water in this desert, there is no electricity. Raju, age 10, explains, 'We had TV in the village, but here we have not seen it for a while. I don't like it when we have a holiday at school because then I do not get to see my friends or watch TV. I feel very lonely. Saturday is half day and Sunday is free, so on Sundays I take a bath, but I always wait for Monday to go to school.'

Munna marches past carrying his oil painting outside, 'If we stay at home we have to work, watch the noisy pump and make sure nothing breaks. You can get hurt. It is much better to come to school. We come when we see the mirror.'

Catching light with a mirror, tent schoolteachers call children to school by focusing light on a distant house. When the kids see the reflecting light they know it is time to come to school. Sounds of voices or school bells are lost in the desert.

134

Chunda, age 10, raises his voice above the crowd because he has some suggestions. 'We have a mirror, but we need another mirror to see how we look and make our hair nice, a drum to sing songs, a cricket bat and ball, and because we have used them all up today – more paints.' Standing up to brush the dust from his faded orange sweatshirt, Chunda continues, 'And more bicycles so everyone can come to school! I come here because otherwise it will be the same old tools, same old digging, same old pump, same old salt.' Chunda walks towards the door and dips out of the tent, announcing, 'Lunchtime!'

Watching The other children collect their tiffin tins and Anji does the same, finding a place to sit in the shade of the sloping side of the tent, opening up her tiffin tin to share her lunch with her friends. Tearing a piece of chapatti, she rolls the soft flatbread in her sun-baked hands and watches thoughtfully, as the wind plays with the edges of her oil painting in the desert.

Ramesh, age 6, his elder brother, Chunda, age 10, and sister, Samta, age 12, ride three on a bicycle to school. They travel six kilometres and it takes them one hour. Ramesh has a red bandage around his ankle because his foot just got caught in the bicycle wheel.

WHEN I GROW UP

I want

'I will make **flowers** I will wear them in my hair and make garlands around my neck,' Reshma Parveen, age 9, Madrasa Masaudhi, Malkana Village, Patna district, Bihar.

Paper

I want to be a

I want to be a

INDIA

'E-mails travel by magic.' Amina, age 14, Mahita Computer Centre, Ganga Dowli, Hyderabad, Andhra Pradesh.

Computer teacher

I want to be

'I would like to have a mango orchard.' Subrat Mohanto, age 8, Sri Aurobindo Purnanga Vidya Pitha, Karanji, Cuttack District, Orissa.

'Every day I used to go to the docks and steal fish when the boats came in. When I grow up I want to be a policeman and catch people like me.' Manoj Sri Durga Mandal, age 11, Ganesh Murti Nagar, Navy Nagar, Mumbai.

Police man

136

to be a

I umpa Das, age 9,
Jabala, Kolkata,
West Bengal.

Dancer

I want to be a

Hafiz

Saidur Rehman,
age 8, Islamia
Muktab, Thicksay,
Leh District,
Ladakh.

'I think I would like
praying all day and
being on the top
of the mountain,'
Jigmat Namdol,
age 6, Tukla
Village,
Leh District,
Ladakh.

monk

I want to be

'I will travel to teach Buddhism ...
doing good things and thinking good
things, don't lie, don't create conflict,
don't harm anybody. And if people
ask what can we really do? Look
at the person nett to you, just
ask them how they
are,' Lobzang Tsultim, age 12,
Chora School, Likeer Gompa
Monastery, Ladakh

I want to be a

Philosopher

Sachin
Tendulkar

'Is my favourite, like him I will be a
batsman. I'd like to score a century,'
Shankar, age 12, Brahmaswam Madam,
Trichur, Trichur District, Kerala.

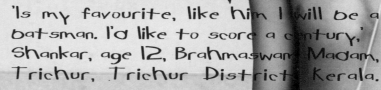

137

I want to be a

teacher

'I'll hang paper cuttings from the ceiling and make more windows so the paper can blow and then play music.' Reshma Ott, age 9, ALP Government School Nochupolly, Mundur, Palghat, Kerala.

gypsy

'I will ride on a camel.' Sukhi, age 8, CRY, Shepherd's development project, Virami village, Pali District, Rajasthan.

भारत
INDIA

Painter

Vicky Kumar, age 10, Pratham school under a tree, Dhabalpura, Patna, Bihar.

Bus Driver

भारत
INDIA

'I will drive people back and forth from my village to Kohima. I'll charge Rs 5, it's the right amount. If you bring chickens I won't charge you extra.' Radi Terhase, age 9, Govt Primary School, Rusoma Village, District Kohima, Nagaland.

Diamond discoverer

'I will be a scientist in Bombay. I want to create medicines so AIDS patients can survive and I'll discover how to make diamonds too.' Ayesha Farek, age 11, Loreto Day School, Kolkata, West Bengal.

'My father puts shoes on horses and buffalos, but I don't want to do that. I want to make two story buildings with slanted roofs.' Shajad, age 7, Madrasa Masaudhi, Malkana Village, Patna district, Bihar.

138

'I want to be a leader to serve the people of India there have been many great leaders in India.' Sanyashi Palei, 10, Gram Vikas High School, Konkia, Ganjam District, Orissa.

'I want to be a saint because I don't like a world where people fight and argue. People are losing faith. I know being a saint will not solve the problem, but it will be not doing what everyone else is doing.' Upendra Mallik, age 12, Gram Vikas High School, Konkia, Ganjam District, Orissa.

saint

'I think that being an Ambassador is the best job because then everyone knows who you are, plus my brother lives in America.' Surabhi, age 12, Patna, Bihar.

Ambassador

I want to be a ?

'Once I went on a train and I saw the conductor, he was wearing long trousers, a pressed shirt and jacket with shiny buttons. I'd like to wear that uniform.' Lochan Buro, age 9.

'I'll help people get down from high steps.' Vimal Joyti Barman, age 9.

'I'd like to see the different places where the land is yellow.' Rup Joyti Deka, age 9, Government Primary School, DPEP, Tengabari Village, Darrang District, Assam.

train men

I want to be a

Girl

Amrita K.M., age 8, ALP Government School Nochupully, Mundur, Palghat District, Kerala.

archeologist

'I will be an archaeologist in Israel. People say Jesus is not real, but I would like to find things to prove he is real. I will look at the ruins and see what can be found. I will take a camera and a small tape recorder, so whatever I discover I can record on my tape.'
Tina Kaviraj, age 11, Loreto Sealdah, Kolkata, West Bengal.

I want to be

'I will teach my mother how to write her name.' Fatima Hashmi, age 9, CREDA Bikna Community Cottage School, ... District, ... Pradesh.

Amitabh Bachchan

'He is my hero,' Sonu, age 9, Pratham school under a tree, Dhabalpura, Patna, Bihar.

'When I am DM I will make sure all children in this district go to school.' Rita Devi, age 9, Bikna Community School, Mirzapur District, UP. CREDA

I want to be a

'street magistrate'

forest ranger

'I will wear a khaki uniform and I will guard the trees because trees must be saved.'

Kailash, age 10, Shiksha Protsahan Kendra, Bhiriyadol Village, Bethu District, MP.

भारत INDIA

'I will swing in the banyan tree's hanging roots where the air is cool and there is a magical breeze.' Kumari Kalyani Muduli, age 10, Sri Aurobindo Purnanga Vidya Pitha, Karanji, Cuttack District, Orissa.

'Famous people live in space with Jupiter, the sun, planets and stars. Robots also live in space with satellites. Shiva lives in space too. I want to fly there and when I see him I would say "oh my god!" and then I would ask him how he made all of the animals. Because that was a really great thing he did.'

I want to be a space explorer

Vikaa Babloo, age [ ] Platinum Jubilee High School, Warangel, AP.

141

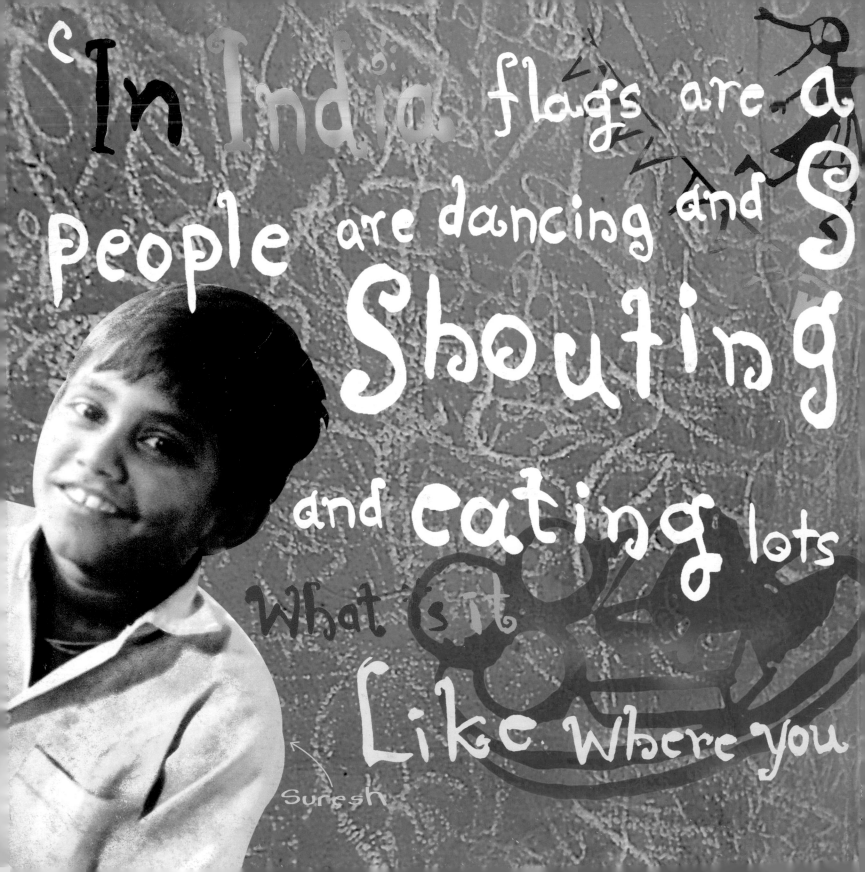

"In India flags are people are dancing and Shouting and eating lots What is it Like where you

Suresh

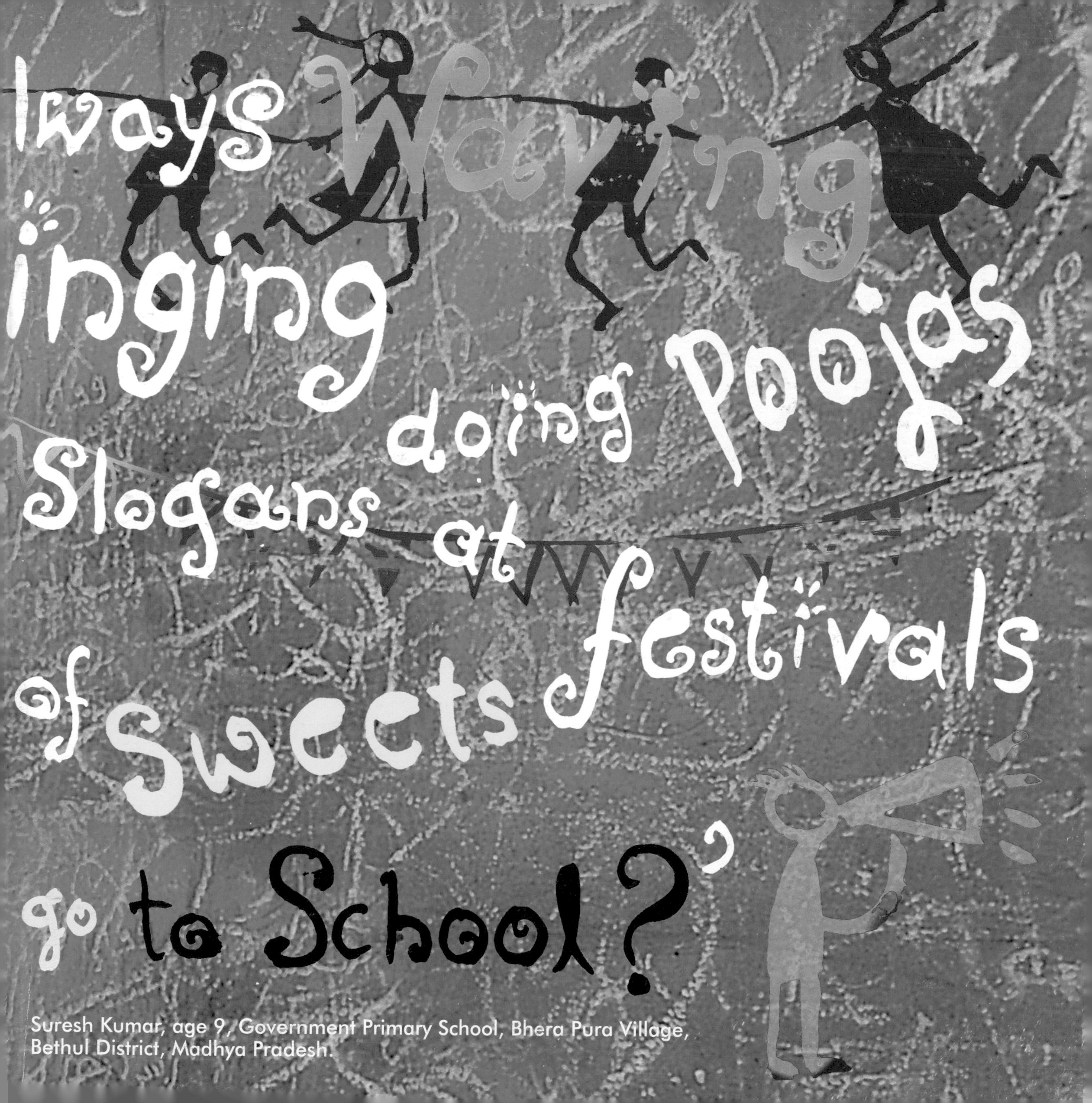

lways Waving

inging

Slogans doing Poojas

of at

Sweets festivals

go to School?'

Suresh Kumar, age 9, Government Primary School, Bhera Pura Village,
Bethul District, Madhya Pradesh.

Millions of children do not go to school in India for many reasons. Many children have to work to help their families survive or stay home to look after their younger brothers and sisters. These children cannot afford the textbooks and pencils they need to go to school. Or quite simply, the nearest school is just too far away to walk to. If these children do try going to school they might find that school is taught in a language they do not understand, they are treated differently because they practice another religion and because they started school too late, they are too far behind to catch up. Many schools in India do not have enough facilities for every child, often there are no ramps for children in wheelchairs, there are no toilets for girls, no drinking water, no electricity, teachers are often absent and the long hours of memorization needed to pass difficult exams make school not a very fun place to be. But against these odds, there are schools, teachers, organizations, parents and children working together to make going to school in India an experience that will change children's lives – for the better. And their stories are here.

Thank You

You hold in your hands a dream that has been made real by extraordinary individuals who believed in what they could not see – a celebration of what school can be.

Thank you, Justine for opening the window, Alana for enduring emotions, Kamath for making our project breathe and Nitin for capturing the light. Many thanks to the Bharti Foundation, Sunil, GK, Hemant and Tina for believing in possibility; to Paramjit for endless changes, Siddhartha for whimsical strategies and Kavita for flair; Hemant, Gautam and Rajiv, trusted trustees; Rajesh for enthusiasm, Sanjay for 'why not', Rahul for details, Chander for the fine print, Cyrus for space to see how far we had come and to Uncle Don for Isadora.

Thank you KK for waving wands, BGVS, Subhash for laughing; Dean, Iqbal, Sharif and Feroz, Save the Children, UK; Augustine, UNICEF Patna; David, UNICEF Delhi; Ayie, Education Department, Government of Nagaland; Anita and Vinod, Anshumala, BGVS; The Wangnoos, Gurkha Houseboats; Madhav, Rukmini, Sanjib and B.K. Das, Pratham; Radha, Mohua and Sonali, CRY; Biraj, Action Aid; Chappal and Mahesh, Mobility India; Yogendra, Bodh; Satyanarayen, VVKS; Inderjit, Khurana, RSSO; Dayaram, EDCIL; Handicap International; Yash from NIEPA who unfortunately will not be able to see how he helped us fly, and to all those who we met along the way, thank you for good directions.

Going to School in India stories have been chosen because they are inspirational and reflect one aspect of India. We visited many more schools in Assam and Nagaland and across India, but unfortunately were unable to create stories from our journey. Our selection by no means passes judgment on the stories, activities, kids and organizations we could not include. This is a 144-page book, to tell a complete story of India would require at least 300 million pages, one for every child, but that book, like India's greatest possibilities, is endless.